Population

AND

Development

Population
AND
Development

A Critical Introduction

Frank Furedi

St. Martin's Press
New York

POPULATION AND DEVELOPMENT

Copyright © Frank Furedi 1997

St. Martin's Press, Scholarly and Reference Division,
175 Fifth Avenue, New York, N.Y. 10010

First published in Great Britain in 1997 by Polity Press

First published in the United States of America in 1997

Printed in Great Britain

ISBN 0-312-17656-2 (cloth)
ISBN 0-312-17658-9 (paper)

Library of Congress Cataloging-in-Publication Data

Furedi, Frank, 1948–
    Population and development / Frank Furedi.
        p.   cm.
    Includes bibliographical references and index.
    ISBN 0-312-17656-2. — ISBN 0-312-17658-9 (pbk.)
    1. Population—Economic aspects. 2. Economic development.
3. Population policy.   I. Title.
    HB849.41.F87   1997
    304.6—dc21   97-16710
                                                            CIP

Contents

Acknowledgements

The author and publishers wish to thank the following for permission to use copyright material:

The Economist for an extract from the 5th May 1994 issue of *The Economist*;

Guardian Newspapers Ltd for an extract from an article by Farida Akter, *The Guardian*, 21st July 1994;

The Population Council for extracts from Geoffrey McNicoll, 'Review of *Beyond the Numbers*', *Population and Development Review*, 20, 3, September 1994, pp. 658, 659;

The World Bank for the table from *Population and Development: Implications for the World Bank*, 1994, p. 21.

Every effort has been made to trace the copyright holders but if any have been inadvertently overlooked the publishers will be pleased to make the necessary arrangement at the first opportunity.

Introduction

In the public mind, population growth is seen as the major cause of problems to do with development today. Poverty in Africa, Asia and Latin America is often blamed on what is called overpopulation. The popular media in particular tends to associate scarcity and famine with a surfeit of mouths to feed.

As somebody involved in the teaching of development studies, I set out to examine the relationship between the problems facing the developing societies of the South and demographic trends. However, in the course of researching this book, I was forced to modify the focus of the study. Closer examination of the subject raised questions about whether there really was a direct link – either negative or positive – between population growth and development. Indeed, it became surprisingly clear that even those specialists who consider population growth to be a fundamental problem of our times, no longer insist on the existence of such a link.

Recent publications of the United Nations Population Fund (UNFPA) treat the relationship between population growth and development as a side issue, and seek to mobilize support for population control programmes on other grounds. Even organizations and individuals who fervently promote programmes designed to curb population growth, now openly acknowledge that there is 'no evidence that population growth is the *cause* of poverty'.[1] Most non-specialist studies of developing societies have not caught up with the changing emphasis in the specialist literature on population, and popular media representations of the issue still associate population growth with problems of economic development, famines and food shortage. However, an important shift of emphasis has taken place, and the more specialist studies, especially those based on empirical research, are far more circumspect. Today, professionals attached to the delivery of population programmes are far more likely to justify their action on the grounds that it will improve women's health or protect the environment, than because it contributes to economic development.

One of the central themes explored in this book is the changing relationship between the discussions of population and development. The shift towards finding new rationales for population policies raises the question of how genuine were previous concerns with the issue of development. One of the most interesting insights gained through a review of the specialist demographic literature and the publications of family planning agencies is that population and development narratives have been diverging for some time. An examination of why this divergence occurred should help to illuminate the uneasy relationship between these issues.

The question of population is not just about numbers. Debates on this subject are highly charged with emotion and carry a heavy ideological baggage. It is often difficult to separate the 'facts' about population from the perceptions of those concerned about the subject. Sometimes the boundary that separates the feeling that there are too many of 'them' and too few of 'us' from a demographic 'fact' is indistinct. Quite often problems that have little to do with demography are experienced or expressed through the prism of population. As one American demographer remarked recently, 'what is called a demographic problem may better be described as a moral and intellectual problem that takes a demographic form.'[2] The possibility that the consciousness of demography may be symptomatic of other anxieties will be explored in subsequent chapters.

Since anxieties about population growth often emerge independently of real demographic trends, it is useful to examine them as a subject in their own right. In chapter 1, this subject – what we might call 'demographic consciousness' – is examined, prior to a wider consideration of the issue of population. This follows what is too often the actual sequence of discussion on the subject. Evidence presented throughout chapters 3 to 6, suggests that fully developed positions about population growth often precede the actual analysis of the problem. And, too frequently, the debate is informed by *a priori* conclusions about the effects of population growth rather than reflections based on the specific analysis of the situation. Consequently, it is often difficult to separate the real workings of demographic trends from their ideological representations. For example, the tension between North and South is clearly expressed through the discussion of demographic issues. Chapter 3 argues that the North–South relationship is a troublesome one, influenced by the themes of power, and military and racial rivalry, rather than simple demographic factors.

Chapters 4 to 6 consider the encounter between development and population growth, reviewing the different stages of the intellectual representation of this encounter. There were three distinct stages in the history of this discussion.

Stage One (1940–55) At the outset, the evolution of the academic discipline of development was directly influenced by emerging apprehensions about the effects of population growth in the South. In this stage – the forties and much of the fifties – development was promoted as a solution to the population problem.

Stage Two (1955–75) The relationship was reversed. More and more, specialists argued that population control was the prerequisite for development. Their contention was that population control would help overcome the obstacles that stood in the way of development

Stage Three (1975–) The link between population and development has diminished in significance. The difficulty of maintaining a plausible linkage between population and development has led to a reorientation of the discussion since the seventies.

Chapter 6 examines the gradual separation of the agenda of population control from the goal of development, which began during the third stage of the discussion. It concludes that the consequence of this process was a shift away from policies designed to encourage development, towards policies designed in the first place to influence attitudes to fertility. This shift implied the Westernization of family values in the South, but without socio-economic change. The policy of what could be called modernization without development remains influential to this day. The attempt to forge a new link – this time between population growth and environmental degradation – is the subject of chapter 8.

Is population growth really a problem? That is a question which recurs time and again throughout this book. Chapter 2 attempts an answer. Often the answers offered by commentators are linked to their wider vision of the world and to their ideological commitments. For example many of the most alarmist accounts of the dangers posed by population growth are motivated by exigencies of military security. And those who oppose population policies are sometimes driven by religious pro-natalist sentiments. At the 1994 International Conference on Population and Development (ICPD) in Cairo, the most vociferous opponents of population control were American conservatives, driven by their hostility to the right of women to abortion. The interweaving of different agendas into the population debate often makes it difficult to understand the different perspectives on the subject. At the outset it is worth examining the main approaches to the population debate today.

Traditionally, writers on the subject have distinguished between those who believe that population growth is a problem and those who do not. In the specialist literature, the pessimistic views on population growth espoused by Thomas Malthus, are often counterposed to the optimistic vision of Karl Marx. As is well known, Malthus believed that if population grew unchecked, the time would come when there would not be enough food to feed people. According to Malthus, population growth threatened the limited resources available to humanity. In contrast, Marx argued that it was not the numbers of people but the way that society was organized which constituted the problem. According to Marx, it was not the limits of nature but of social organization which accounted for hunger and poverty. This clash of views continues to influence the many debates on the consequences of population growth. But the Malthus–Marx controversy does not provide an adequate intellectual framework for assessing the debate of the late twentieth century. Not surprisingly, the nineteenth century clash of views about the relationship between population, natural resources and society has developed in a number of new directions.

It is not particularly helpful to situate the contemporary population controversy in terms of the classical Malthus-Marx debate. The discussion today does not even fit into the classical ideological pattern. For example, China, whose government claims to adhere to Marxist principles, vigorously advocates its one-child policy and is in the forefront of promoting population control. At the same time some anti-Marxist economists, who uphold the virtues of the free market, strongly oppose population programmes. They believe that food and other shortages can be corrected by economic incentives and the workings of the free market. Their hostility to population programmes is shaped by their dislike of state intervention.

A wide variety of views are expressed in the contemporary population debate. The most influential views – eight in all – are considered below. These approaches are not necessarily mutually exclusive. For example those associated with the population lobby – professionals involved with organizations like UNFPA, the Population Council, the International Planned Parenthood Federation (IPPF) – often shift from one approach to another. Of the eight approaches considered below, the first six believe that population growth constitutes some kind of a problem. The last two contend that there is no population problem.

1 *The Developmentalist Perspective*. Until the nineties, this was one of the most influential perspectives. Its advocates argue that rapid population growth represents a major obstacle to development, as valuable resources are diverted from productive expenditure to the feeding of a growing population. Some also contend that development in turn solves the problem of population. They believe that increasing prosperity and the modernization of lifestyles will create a demand for smaller families, leading to the stabilization of population growth. A classical account of this approach can be found in Coale and Hoover (1958). It is worth noting that at least until the early eighties, this was the most prominent argument used by many leading demographers and most of the influential promoters of population control. These perspectives are discussed in chapters 4 and 5.

2 *The Redistributionist Perspective*. Those who uphold the redistributionist perspective are sceptical of the view that population growth directly causes poverty and underdevelopment. They often interpret high fertility as not so much the cause but the effect of poverty. Why? Because poverty, lack of economic security, the high mortality rates of children, the low status of women and other factors force people to have large families. They also believe that population is a problem because it helps to intensify the impoverishment of the masses. For some redistributionists, the solution to the problem lies in changing the status of poor people, particularly of women, through education and reform. Repetto (1979) and the World Bank (1984) provide a clear statement of this approach. This perspective is linked to the Women and Human Rights approach

discussed below. Some proponents of redistribution contend that the population problem can only be solved through far-reaching social reform. (See Sen and Grown (1988) for a radical version of the redistributionist argument.) Chapter 7 gives an overview of this feminized perspective.

3 *The Limited Resources Perspective.* This perspective represents the synthesis of traditional Malthusian concern about natural limits with the preoccupation of contemporary environmentalism. According to the limited resources perspective, population growth has a negative and potentially destructive impact on the environment. Its proponents argue that even if a growing population can be fed, the environment cannot sustain such large numbers; population growth will lead to the explosion of pollution, which will have a catastrophic effect on the environment. See Harrison (1993) for a clear statement of this position. Chapter 8 surveys this perspective.

4 *The Socio-Biological Perspective.* This approach politicizes the limited resources perspective. Its proponents present population growth as a threat not only to the environment but also to a way of life. They regard people as polluters and often define population growth as a pathological problem. In the West, the ruthless application of this variant of Malthusianism leads to demands for immigration control. Some writers call for the banning of foreign aid to the countries of the South, on the grounds that its stimulates an increase in the rate of fertility. Other writers believe that the numbers of people threatens the ecosystem, and even go so far as to question the desirability of lowering the rate of infant mortality.[3] Abernethy (1993) and Hardin (1993) provide a systematic presentation of the socio-biological perspective.

5 *The People-as-a-Source-of-Instability Perspective.* In recent years, contributions on international relations have begun to discuss population growth in terms of its effect on global stability. Some writers have suggested that in the post-Cold War order, the growth of population has the potential to undermine global stability. Some see the rising expectations of large numbers of frustrated people as the likely source of violent protest and a stimulus for future wars and conflicts. The key theme they emphasize is the differential rate of fertility between the North and the South. From this perspective the high fertility regime of the South represents a potential threat to the fast-ageing population of the North. (See Kennedy (1993)).[4]

6 *The Women and Human Rights Perspective.* This perspective associates a regime of high birth rates with the denial of essential

human rights. Those who advocate this approach insist that the subordination of women and their exclusion from decision making has kept birth rates high. Some suggest that because of their exclusion from power and from access to safe reproductive technology, many women have more children then they otherwise would wish. The importance of gender equality for the stabilization of population is not only supported by feminist contributors but by significant sections of the population movement. At the Cairo Conference of 1994, this perspective was widely endorsed by the main participants. For a clear exposition of this approach see Correa (1994) and Sen, Germain and Chen (1994).

7 *The People-as-Problem-Solvers Perspective.* In contrast to the approaches mentioned so far, this one does not believe that population growth constitutes a problem. On the contrary, its advocates believe that the growth of population has the potential to stimulate economic growth and innovation. From this perspective, more people means more problem solvers, since human creativity has the potential to overcome the limits of nature. Some believe that in the final analysis, the market mechanism can help to establish a dynamic equilibrium between population growth and resources. Others emphasize the problem-solving abilities of the human mind. See Boserup (1993) and Simon (1981) for illustrations of this approach.

8 *The Religious Pro-Natalist Perspective.* Some of the most vocal opponents of population policy are driven by religious objections to any interference with the act of reproduction. They argue that population growth is not a problem and are deeply suspicious of any attempt to regulate fertility. Although some supporters of this perspective mobilize economic arguments to support their case, the relationship between population growth and development is incidental to their argument. For them, the argument that population growth is positive is in the first instance justified on religious grounds. See Kasun (1988) for a clear exposition of this perspective. Other pro-natalist voices regard the growth of the population of the South as a positive asset that will contribute to a more equitable relation of power with the North. They view population programmes as an insidious attempt to maintain Western domination. (See IPFA (1995)).

Not every contribution on the subject can be fitted neatly into one of the above perspectives. Many writers adopt a number of perspectives and shift from one to another during the course of debate. Most serious contributors are open to the need to modify their conclusions. Indeed, one of the reasons why the alleged link between population growth and poverty has been undermined is that some proponents of this view were prepared to accept the results of research which contradicted their assumptions. There are also important contributors who do not fit into any of the categories. For example, some writers are population sceptics; they question a lot of the arguments made on behalf of the stabilization of fertility, but nevertheless still feel that something should be done to limit numbers. (See Hartmann (1987)).

The aim of this text is not to advocate a particular theory of population growth. Its main concern is to examine why so many different problems are now viewed in connection with population. The central theme is to analyse the manner in which the relationship between population growth and development has been conceptualized, fought out and altered. The book takes neither a positive nor a negative view of population growth itself. Unlike the perspectives outlined above, the argument here is that population growth is not a subject that can be understood in its own terms. Demographic patterns are subject to numerous influences, and do not *a priori* work towards inexorable conclusions. The most critical demographic changes in this century – the fall of mortality rates in the South and the collapse of fertility rates in Europe – were not anticipated by most experts. Nor can the consequences of population growth be determined in advance. The effects of population growth will be decided through a process of interaction with the prevailing socio-economic structures and cultural practices. To label the consequences of population growth as 'bad' or 'good' is to lose sight of the wider social perspective.

What effect population growth has always depends on the specific circumstances that prevail in the societies under examination. For example, falling birth rates in Britain and Europe have not increased employment opportunities for people, but have, for a variety of reasons, coincided with high levels of unemployment. At the same time, there is a labour shortage in many of Asia's leading economies, even though this region has higher rates of fertility. This difference in economic fortune between two parts of the world has little to do with the rhythm of population growth. It has a lot to do with the ability of the two respective societies to productively employ the talents of their people today.

When they seek to project a particular demographic pattern into the indefinite future, theories of population growth have proved to be spectacular failures. The irrelevance of past predictions which warned of populations dying out or of demographic timebombs exploding, should encourage a degree of healthy scepticism on this subject. Maybe it is time to interrogate this powerful contemporary consciousness of demography. What are the underlying issues that have stimulated such an obsessive engagement with the issue of population growth? What problems have discussions on population size really been seeking to address? Is the population lobby centrally concerned with development and poverty – or are these issues merely incidental to the main agenda?

1

The Numbers Game

The population of the world is nearly 5.7 billion. According to projections from the United Nations, it is likely to increase to around 7.6 billion by the year 2015. It is generally recognized that population growth rates have begun to slow around the world, including many developing countries. Nevertheless, it is suggested that many developing countries will still continue to experience large absolute increases in population. According to the World Bank, the populations of the countries of the South 'are expected to increase by more people during the 1990s than during any previous decade' (World Bank, 1995, p. 22). This increase is due to what demographers call population momentum, which results in many more births than deaths. It is the product of the combination of continued high fertility rates and youthful age structures in developing societies.

The size of a population and its variation are affected by three factors: fertility rates, mortality rates and rates of migration. In the contemporary discussion of population growth most attention focuses on birth rates.

During the past forty years most of the significant increases in population have been in the South. However there are substantial variations in the factors influencing the growth of national or regional populations. For example, during the 1980s, national fertility averages ranged from an estimated 8.5 children per woman in Rwanda to 1.3 in Italy. More recent figures, for 1994, show that the differences continue: in sub-Saharan Africa in 1994, women averaged 6.5 children each, compared to only 1.6 in Western Europe. In contrast to the South, the population of the industrial world has also grown older, tending to slow the growth in population size, with the potential for even a contraction in some regions.

Table 1 indicates that during the period 1950–90, the largest absolute increases in population took place in Asia, where almost six out of every ten of the world's people now live. During this period, the population of Africa nearly tripled. At the same time the population of Europe and the former Soviet Union, while still growing absolutely, fell as a percentage of the world's population from twenty-three to fifteen per cent.

TABLE 1 POPULATION AND PERCENTAGE DISTRIBUTION, BY GEOGRAPHIC REGION 1950–90					
	POPULATION – MILLIONS			PERCENTAGE OF WORLD POPULATION		
Region	1950	1970	1990	1950	1970	1990
World	2,516	3,697	5,267	100.0	100.0	100.0
Less industrial countries	1,684	2,648	4,052	66.9	71.7	76.9
More industrial countries	832	1,049	1,215	33.1	28.3	23.1
Africa	222	363	628	8.9	9.8	11.9
East Africa	98	162	274	3.9	4.4	5.2
West Africa	72	118	214	2.9	3.2	4.1
North Africa	52	83	140	2.1	2.2	2.6
America	331	510	715	13.2	13.8	13.6
Latin America and Caribbean	165	284	435	6.6	7.7	8.3
North America	166	226	280	6.6	6.1	5.3
Asia	1,376	2,102	3,107	54.7	56.9	59.0
East and Southeast Asia	853	1,274	1,788	33.9	34.5	34.0
South Asia	481	754	1,186	19.1	20.4	22.5
Southwest Asia	42	74	133	1.7	2.0	2.5
Europe and USSR	572	703	790	22.7	19.0	15.0
Oceania	13	27	0.5	0.5	0.5	0.5

Source: World Bank, Population and Development: Implications for the World Bank, 1994, p. 21.

These figures emphasize the variations in population growth rates. The growing divergence between the population shares of the less industrial and more industrial worlds is likely to continue. In 1990, four out of every five people lived in the developing countries. The World Bank estimates that in 2100, that ratio will be closer to ten out of every eleven people (1995, p. 28).

1.1 Competitive Fertility

The trends outlined above have prompted widespread discussion about the 'population problem'. However, what people mean by a population problem is far from self-evident. At any one time, for example, the significance attached to the rate of fertility appears to be influenced by the particular preoccupation of the interpreter. Sometimes commentators are alarmed by high fertility and the `population explosion' in Africa, at other times they are troubled by the fall in the rate of births in the West. `Is the West heading for extinction?' asked a columnist in the London *Evening Standard*.[1] Such questions invariably invite comparisons with the rate of fertility of other societies. These comparisons are expressed most clearly in the vocabulary of competitive fertility.

Like many other forms of competition – economic, political, military – that of competitive fertility is linked to considerations of power. The consciousness of competitive fertility is most prominent in societies where rival communities eye each other's numbers with suspicion. For example during the 1995 referendum on the issue of independence for Quebec, Lucien Bouchard, the leader of the French Canadian separatist movement, remarked that 'we're one of the white races that has the fewest children'.[2] For Bouchard the rate of fertility of French Canadian women was a vital component in his struggle with English-speaking Canada. In many other countries – from India to Nigeria – competing ethnic and religious groups regard differential levels of fertility as a matter crucial to their survival. The theme of competitive fertility also exists at the global level of North–South relations. To this day the motif of competitive fertility influences considerations of demography.

Often those who would like to peg back population growth within other groups or societies are apprehensive about the fall in birth rates within their own. For example, during the 1970s, Russian planners and Western Sovietologists began to express concern over the high birth rate of Muslims in the Soviet Union. They feared that, if prevailing demographic trends persisted, the Soviet Union would become a majority Muslim nation in the 21st century (Rashid, 1994, p. 56). In the same way, observers have interpreted the contemporary decline of the population in Russia as symptomatic of a society 'nervous about the future'.[3] The fall in the number of children born to each Russian woman, from an average of 2.17 in 1989 to 1.4 today, has been characterized as a major demographic crisis.

Discussions on the falling rate of population in Europe highlight the different standards that seem to be applied in the population discussion. For example, the European Union promotes population control policies abroad. Yet at the same time it expresses concern about the fact that Europeans now constitute a declining proportion of the world's population – in other words, there are too few young Europeans and they are procreating at too low a rate. A resolution adopted by the European Parliament in 1983 noted 'that population trends in Europe will have a decisive effect on the development of Europe and will determine the significance of the role which Europe will play in the world in future decades'.[4] In Europe and the United States, many writers have warned about the negative consequences of an ageing population and have suggested that there may be too few young productive workers to support a growing number of pensioners. In contrast, writers often describe the population problem in the South in terms of there being not too few, but too many young people. They contend that the rising number of young people in the South provides a potential source of instability and stress; in the words of one American diplomat, the youth of these societies are considered particularly 'susceptible to extremism, terrorism and violence' (Kasun, 1988, p. 56).

The prevalence of a differential attitude, which sees a youthful population as desirable in the North but not in the South, suggests that what is at stake here is not a neutral discussion about numbers in the abstract. Statements about numbers are often driven by another agenda, which is not readily apparent. A brief review of the issues to which discussions of population size have attached themselves during the past two centuries may help to place the changing narrative of demography in perspective.

1.2 Themes in Demographic Discourse

Malthus' famous statement, that 'population, when unchecked, increases in a geometrical ratio' but 'subsistence increases only in an arithmetical ratio' is often cited in the contemporary literature on population. What is less often considered is that Malthus was not primarily interested in the question of population itself. The development of a specific theory of population was, on the whole, incidental to Malthus' central objectives (1970, p. 71).[5] First and foremost, his denunciation of population growth was informed by his opposition to the programme of social reform.

Malthus' 'Essay', written in 1798, was a reaction against the optimistic vision of humanity offered by Enlightenment thinkers. Authors such as Condorcet and Godwin argued that human misery was the product of defective social institutions; for Godwin, social reform held out the prospect of the perfectibility of human beings. Malthus rejected this approach. He argued that welfare measures like the English Poor Laws merely intensified impoverishment, since they allowed the poor to breed more. According to Malthus, any benefits from social reforms would be cancelled out by the consequent increase in fertility, since a larger population would have less food and resources. He mobilized the arguments about the dangers of population growth as weapons in his battle of ideas against social reform.

Malthus argued that the obstacles presented by nature would destroy attempts to improve the position of humanity. During the nineteenth century, his influence was limited by the prevailing trends in society. The powerful dynamic of economic development contradicted the pessimistic view of human potential contained in the Malthusian account. To most observers, it seemed that human ingenuity could overcome many of the limits set by nature. During this period of industrial expansion, the dominant theme was not so much the fear of overpopulation as panics about underpopulation. From the industrial revolution until the 1960s, pro-natalism – the encouragement of high birth rates – was the predominant influence in Western societies. Governments and opinion-makers associated prosperity and military security with growing numbers. In contrast to Malthus, they were troubled by any signs of a slow-down in the rate of fertility and had no worries about overpopulation.

Another potent source of pro-natalist sentiment was the development of racism. In nineteenth-century Europe the influence of racial thinking encouraged positive views about population growth. It was widely believed that strong races were by definition fertile races. Fertility was also linked with positive moral qualities. In contrast, decadent or declining races were generally represented as infertile. This perspective led many influential interwar American demographers to such curious conclusions as that blacks could not reproduce in an urban environment.[6] Such sentiments were part of the legacy of Social Darwinism, and its emphasis on the survival of the 'fittest' race.

SOCIAL DARWINISM ON FERTILITY

For Social Darwinists, the people of the world are not only different. As races, they also exist at different levels of human evolution. The advent of Darwinism in the 1860s coincided with an outburst of interest in Europe in racial differences. One interpretation of Darwin's theory of evolution – that of Social Darwinism – was to link the chain of development from ape to human with prevailing racial theories of inherent difference and inferiority. From this standpoint, certain 'primitive ' people were represented as early historical forms. For Social Darwinists, this hierarchy of people was seen to be the product of natural selection. Through the process of selection, the fittest races and people rose to the top. In this theory, biological and social success were intertwined. In contrast, less successful or inferior people suffered from biological decline. Ultimately they were threatened with extinction.

During the nineteenth century, the concern with differential fertility was very much bound up with the Social Darwinist notion of power. For Social Darwinists, superiority was linked to the power to reproduce. As Britain's Walter Bagehot argued (1872, p. 195), 'the most successful races, other things being equal, are those which multiply the fastest.' High rates of fertility were not only seen as symptoms of racial vitality, but also as essential for the exercise of global power. Although Social Darwinism fell into disrepute in the interwar period, European governments continued to regard falling birth rates as a major challenge to their global position. For example, in 1937, Britain's House of Commons resolved that the 'tendency of population to decline may well be a danger to the maintenance of the British Empire'. It also set up a Royal Commission on the subject (Symonds and Carder, 1973, p. 6).

A fecund, virile race was also seen as a guarantee of military security. That is why apprehensions about military security were often interpreted in demographic terms – Prussia's victory over France in 1871 was widely blamed on the stagnation of the French population. In subsequent decades, the fall in population in France was often characterized as a sign of 'national degeneracy' or 'national feebleness', the decline in French fertility experienced as an 'evil sapping the vitality of the nation' (Teitelbaum and Winter, 1985, p. 30 and pp. 17–21). This sentiment also dominated academic thinking in the USA at the turn of the century. For example in 1907, Edward Ross, one of the central figures of early American sociology, argued for a package of policies which included encouraging 'capable' people to have children, imposing birth control on the 'overprolific people', and curbing immigration. In the language of his time, he summoned up a vision of an impending biological war:

> Numbers tell. France dreads prolific Germany. Germany trembles before yet more prolific Russia. Europe fears the awakening of the teaming yellow race. In South Africa the whites stand aghast at the rabbit-like increase of the blacks. Until backward mankind has clambered up, or been lifted up, from the animal plane, the sunny spots created by scientific industry coupled with prudent parentage will be menaced by an influx, peaceful or armed, from the crowded areas, and the bristling frontiers between peoples and races will have to remain.[7]

Today many experts echo Ross, combining arguments about the inability of Western society to absorb economic migrants with calls for population control.

In Britain, too, population growth was once associated with positive racial characteristics. Many imperial thinkers argued that the maintenance of the British Empire required a steady increase in the population of the 'English' race. With the onset of a fall in the rate of population growth – new parents in the 1900s had only half as many children as their own parents – many expressed concern for the future of the Empire. 'The British nations overseas are already underpopulated, and if these nations are to remain of British stock, they must either check their falling birth rates or attract young settlers from the Mother Country', wrote one advocate of pro-natalist policies (Sutherland, 1994, p. 32). Apprehension about the maintenance of the British Empire led directly to the establishment of a Royal Commission on Population in 1937. The motive of stimulating the fertility and the quality of the British race also informed the deliberations regarding the establishment of the Welfare State. 'With its present rate of reproduction the British race cannot continue; means of reversing the recent course of the birth-rate must be found', reported William Beveridge, the main author of the proposals that led to the establishment of the Welfare State (cited in Sutherland, 1944, p. 17). Beveridge hoped that improvement in the provision of welfare would contribute to the amelioration of the British stock.

During the interwar period, fears about imperial decline converged with a strong sense of insecurity about the trajectory of the world economy. Many experts blamed economic stagnation and the coming of the Great Depression on the stagnant rates of birth in the West. During this period, most economists and demographers defined the population problem as one of falling birth rates. The renowned British economist, John Maynard Keynes, informed the Eugenics Society in February 1937 that the problem of overpopulation had been solved and that, instead, society was 'threatened by another danger'. This danger was the 'deficiency of demand' caused by the low stagnant rate of birth (Overbeek, 1974, p. 142). Policy-makers sought ideas on how to encourage married couples to have larger families. This conceptual linkage between population decline and economic stagnation remained influential until the end of Second World War.

Concern with population decline was not merely with its quantity but also with its quality. As Grebnik noted; 'the fact that the birth rate has fallen more steeply among the upper than among the lower sections of the population, coupled with a somewhat naive identification of social and economic success with higher biological value provoked growing alarm in some quarters that the quality of population was deteriorating'.[8] According to one account, some among the British social elite had an 'obsessive concern' with the birth rate of the lower classes. Worried about the quality of the population, they implicitly linked physical deterioration with moral inferiority. The belief that large sections of the lower classes were 'unfit' coincided with the recognition that this section of the British race reproduced far faster then the more solid middle classes. The fear that the lower classes would outbreed the rest and contribute to the degeneration of the race helped foster a climate

EUGENICS

In 1883, Charles Darwin's cousin, the British scientist Francis Galton, coined the term eugenics. Eugenics was presented as the science of improving the human stock by promoting superior people and races over the less 'suitable' ones. Because of the Nazi experience and its asssociation with human sociobiology, eugenics has fallen into disrepute. Today, arguments proposing the improvement of populations are rarely expressed in a direct form.

where eugenic views could flourish. From the eugenic point of view the problem was not the level of population growth as such, but the tendency for the lower – and by implication morally inferior – classes to increase at a faster rate than the middle class.

Eugenic sentiments also developed in the United States, where fears of blacks breeding faster than whites and of immigrants overwhelming the Anglo-Saxon population were widespread. The higher fertility rates of most immigrants relative to 'indigenous' Americans was a frequent subject of discussion until the Second World War. It is worth noting that anxieties regarding the possible demise of the American character stimulated the publication of some of the earliest work in American demography (See Teitelbaum and Winter, 1985, p. 50). For those who advocated the eugenic cause, the solution was to limit the fertility of the 'unfit' and to increase the birth rate of the 'fit'. Population control was specifically targeted at those held responsible for the 'deterioration' of the race. Eugenic arguments expressed a sense of isolation and insecurity among sections of the ruling classes in the West. Such sentiments were motivated by the fear that, through the sheer weight of their numbers, the 'wrong' kind of people would overwhelm the respectable citizenry. These fears were always oriented towards a particular section of the population. When the British Eugenics Society set up a Population Policies Committee in 1938, because of its concern with declining birth rates, its aim was not to increase fertility at random but to 'improve the reproductive power of the eugenically good in different occupational groups' (Jones, 1986, p. 130).

A concern with the 'right' or 'wrong' type of person – with the quality rather than simply the quantity of population – is still in evidence to this day. In recent years, the discovery of the so-called underclass in the inner cities of Britain and the USA, with its culture of crime and dependency, has been used to attack the irresponsible reproductive behaviour of single mothers. Charles Murray, one of the leading proponents of this thesis, has warned that in Britain 'illegitimacy has been sky-rocketing since 1979 (1990, p. 5). For conservatives like Murray, an explosion in the number of offspring of 'illegitimate' unions is not only a problem of numbers, but of what kind of people are being born. Underclass theorists regard the growth of population not only from the quantitative but also the qualitative side. From their perspective illegitimacy tends to breed people with qualities that can only exacerbate the problems of society.

Roy Calne's *Too Many People* (1994) eloquently expresses an elitist vision of a nightmare scenario, where too many of the wrong kind of people threaten the integrity of society. According to Calne, 'looting and widespread street violence can erupt, spreading widely from the underclass to all strata of the community.' This fear of the many acquires panic-like proportions when the 'population bomb' in Africa is considered. Here 'numerous pathetic mothers, infants and children predominate in the scenes of this obscene tragedy . . . How much better if birth control had prevented their conception rather than for them to be killed by starvation after two or three years of miserable life', sighs Calne (1994). Such strong reactions to the reproductive behaviour of the lower orders – be they European or African – invokes a strident moral message. Single mothers in the inner cities of the West are indicted alongside the peasant communities of Africa and Asia. The tone of moral condemnation can always be found in Western criticism of African fertility. According to one account, 'loose family structures are largely responsible for the world's highest birth rates' which in turn have encouraged an 'anarchic implosion of criminal violence' in the African continent.[9]

The relationship between fear of numbers and racial motifs is an ambivalent one. Quantitative and qualitative concerns with population exist in a dynamic relation with each other. From the first, the relationship between population studies and fears of an increase in the wrong type of people invited arguments about what was the matter with these people. Social Darwinist and eugenic explanations were already at the disposal of those who sought to explain the inferiority of the poor in Europe. Similar explanations were deployed about inferior people in the colonies. For example, the British economist, Alfred Marshall's treatment of differential fertility targeted both the domestic poor and the 'inferior' races abroad:

> if the lower classes of Englishmen multiply more rapidly than those which are morally and physically superior, not only will the population of England deteriorate, but also that part of the population of America and Australia which descends from Englishmen will be less intelligent than it otherwise would be. Again if Englishmen multiply less rapidly than the Chinese, this spiritless race will overrun portions of the earth that otherwise would have been peopled by English vigour. (Cited in Jones, 1986, p. 145.)

Marshall's concern with the inverse relationship between social status and fertility combined both the quantitative and qualitative

aspects of the problem. Such considerations became central to the
development of population studies.

Initially the focus of population theory was on the differential
growth rates of groups of people within one society. Even in the
thirties and forties, population theory was explicitly concerned
with eugenic themes. The main focus of the literature was on the
problem that 'fertility and social status are, and have been in-
versely related.' American social scientists warned about the
consequences of the trend 'whereby the people who are presumably the most valuable have much smaller families than those
of less value'.[10] According to a contribution on the intellectual
history of American demography, 'the principal interest for American demographers until well into the 1930s continued to be the
eugenics-inspired project of tracing domestic fertility differentials
between classes and races.'[11] Notions of superiority and inferiority
were implicit in this literature. It was only a matter of time before
this focus on fertility differentials inside the United States shifted
to the plane of international relations.

From the discussion to date, it should be clear that anxieties
about the growth of a specific population can coexist with apprehension about the falling level of fertility of another. The fears of
population decline and of population growth evolved in tandem
until 1945. From this period onwards, however, apprehension
about population growth became the dominant current in demographic discussions in the West. There were two reasons for this
outcome. The horrors of the Nazi experience had undermined the
eugenic tradition. Thus, in Western societies, it was difficult to
implement policies which explicitly sought to 'improve' the quality of the race or to increase the rate of fertility. The second
influence was the growing perception that the differential rate of
fertility between the North and the South was working against the
industrialized world. During the forties, the problem of domestic
fertility differentials paled into insignificance as compared to the
discussion of the population explosion in the South. Once
competitive fertility was seen to work against the West, the
population growth of the Third World soon emerged as the problem.
This was not the product of some malevolent conspiracy but of the
convergence of pre-existing sentiments about differential fertility
and the unfolding geopolitical realities.

A strong consciousness of differential fertility explains the enduring influence of competitive fertility on considerations of the
demographic issue. Chapter 3 deals at length with the role of

competitive fertility in North–South relations, but here a few words about the relationship of geopolitics and demographic consciousness are in order. It is the demand for security that gives demography a geopolitical dimension. As Teitelbaum and Winter argue 'perceptions of threats to nation, class, or race' are often 'expressed in demographic form' (1985, p. 17). Until the post-war period, the sentiment that numerical superiority was crucial for survival influenced societies throughout the world. The view that some form of biological rivalry underpinned human conflict had many subscribers among military leaders. The fear of being outnumbered has created and continues to create an interest in strategic demography. It is worthy of note that the CIA has recently taken a fresh interest in the relationship between population growth and the question of security.[12] Similar sentiments have also been expressed by Russian nationalist politicans, who are worried by what they consider to be unfavourable demographic realities on their Eastern border.

Those writers who are interested in strategic demography represent the differential rate of fertility between the North and the South as one of the key issues of our time. For some time now, experts in strategic demography have identified the differential rate of fertility growth as a source of danger to Western security. The American academic Phyllis Piotrow put the argument thus: 'Wherever juxtaposed groups experience different fertility rates, the group with the highest per capita income and the greatest economic power is always the group with the lowest fertility. In these circumstances population growth represents a threat to the status quo: to political dominance and economic and social stability. This threat can easily erupt into a political crisis' (cited in IPFA, 1995, p. 46). The theme of population growth as a threat to the status quo retains its salience in a world where a low fertility, prosperous North coexists with a higher fertility, poor South. That is why, as Donaldson pointed out, American political leaders have 'ranked population growth behind only nuclear war as the second most important threat to the world' (P. J. Donaldson, 1990, p. ix).

Since the end of the Cold War, strategic demography has acquired a steady momentum. Numerous European observers have identified 'the unprecedented demographic growth of the population of the South' as the central threat to global security. Others stress the population crisis of the North as the key problem. 'The demographic crisis in the northern hemisphere is already having serious effects on security issues' argued Yves Boyer to a symposium on the subject of *Population Change and European Security*.[13] Fears about security are often linked to perceptions of an impending mass influx of migrants from the South.

The more alarmist accounts present population growth as a direct threat to the Western way of life. Differential fertility not only has quantitative but also qualitative consequences. Paul Kennedy's *Preparing For the Twenty-First Century* posits demographic trends as the key problem facing the West. Kennedy states that these trends call into question the survival of Western values. How, he asks, can these values 'maintain their prevailing position in a world overwhelmingly peopled by societies which did not experience the rational scientific and liberal assumptions of the Enlightenment' (1993, p. 46)? This analysis links differential rates of fertility to a clash of values or culture. For Kennedy, the population growth of the South helps to undermine the global influence of the West.

Those who view the world from the perspective of strategic demography regard the stabilization of the population of the South as a precondition for international security. Yet arguments for population control are rarely posed in explicitly geopolitical terms. Population policies tend to be justified on the grounds that they will help raise the living standard of the poor. This is not surprising since an explicit acknowledgement of security concerns would highlight the conflictual relationship between Western elites and the targets of population policy. That is why Malthusian arguments linking population growth to poverty tend to be favoured over geopolitical ones. The association of the issue of economic development with that of demographic concerns was, at least in part, motivated by the desire to contain the conflictual dynamic. It will be considered in chapter 4.

One of the main contentions of this book is that the growth of academic ideas about encouraging the economic development of the societies of Africa, Asia and Latin America was at least in part inspired by the non-economic motive of avoiding the consequences of a population explosion in the South. It is important to realize that many of the proponents of economic growth regarded the South as a potential threat and saw development as an instrument to contain the danger. This instrumentalist approach to development was motivated by the desire to preserve the global status quo. Many writers were prepared to make economic concessions to the South in exchange for good demographic behaviour. This standpoint was eloquently argued by W. S. Thompson, arguably one of the most influential American analysts of international demographic trends (1946). It was as if demographic experts believed that economic growth would help prevent the population disease of the South from spreading to the North. Often such sentiments were expressed in a benevolent, even humanitarian form. For example, in 1943, the American liberal Bruno Lasker wrote that the 'sin which we and other economically strong nations have committed against the weaker and more populous ones, is not that we have prevented them from sharing our homeland but that we have prevented them from making the most of their own'.[14] Years before the Kennedy administration insisted on helping the people of the Third World 'help themselves', it was implicit in mid-century demography that economic growth in places like Asia was America's best guarantee against mass immigration.

Aid was the price to be paid for defusing the population bomb. One demand for assistance to be given the Third World was justified in the following terms:

> These peoples are problems, even hazards, for all of the countries of the world as endemic and epidemic diseases, as areas of economic dependency, as explosive centres of unrest and rebellion and as possible disturbers of world peace if and when they should attempt the age-old nostrum of alleviating their population pressure by aggressive action against presumably more favourably situated peoples. It is desirable, in fact essential, that they be extricated from their adverse state at the earliest possible moment (Hertzler, 1956, p. 111).

Such sentiments, which viewed 'population pressure' as a potential plague threatening Western societies, were regularly published in the American media in the post-1945 period. Aid and development were represented as a means of checking the multitudinous South.

A profound consciousness of limits is another theme that is consistently prominent in the literature on demography. From Malthus to today, there has developed an intellectual tradition which believes that human action is limited by the obstacles posed by nature. Sometimes, this approach assumes an environmentalist form – today, problems of the environment are often blamed on population growth (see chapter 7). A review of the history of demographic debates indicates that this sense of limits often tends to coincide with a general climate of pessimism regarding future possibilities. Today, the sense of limits exists in a particularly developed form. Some environmentalists now profess a strongly sceptical view of humanity. Humans are seen as destroyers of the environment, depicted as a negative force that punishes and pollutes the earth. More humans merely intensify this act of destruction. Such views explicitly or at least implicitly question the premise of the classical humanist outlook. A Malthusian doctor has written recently that 'hitherto, living man has been the measure of all things; now many people are beginning to wonder if this measure should not be the integrity of the ecosystem'.[15] Others too have questioned the humanist world-view. Moore Lappé and Schurman have criticized the humanist philosophical premise. They question Simon's optimistic perspective on the grounds that 'it implies that the impact of population growth can be judged solely as to how it affects human well-being, ignoring any responsibility toward the integrity of the larger ecosphere' (see Moore Lappé and Schurman, 1989, p. 9). By shifting the focus to beyond human well-being, new arguments can be mobilized against the growth of population.

AN ALL-PURPOSE CAUSE OF PROBLEMS

During the past two hundred years a variety of problems have been blamed on population growth. Population growth has been among the things blamed for:

- famine
- poverty
- instability and revolution
- the spread of Communism
- failure of Third World economies
- environmental degradation
- the domination of women

It should be clear by now that a wide variety of distinct concerns are being interpreted through the medium of demography. At various times it has been argued that population growth was responsible for poverty and famine, for environmental degradation, for the spread of Communism or the political disintegration of the African continent. The definition of the problems changes with the fashion, it is just the concern with population growth which endures. Just as eugenics provided a biological language through which anxieties about social instability could be expressed, so demography offers a vocabulary for making sense of different forms of conflict.

Concerns about population decline and population explosions express a social mood as much as anything else. As the British demographer Carr-Saunders observed, it is not so much the reality of overpopulation but 'the belief that it exists' which influences action. While the reasons offered for the problematizing of population have changed, the demand for a narrative which stigmatizes demographic growth has remained constant. It seems that this obsession with population growth, independent of real demographic trends, is itself a subject worthy of investigation.

1.3 A Silent Discourse

Much, though by no means all of demographic debate appears to be influenced by a fear of being outnumbered. It is often shaped by the sentiment that the 'wrong' kind of people are reproducing too fast. Such emotions and reactions are today rarely expressed openly, since they touch on highly sensitive matters. Moreover, since the end of the Second World War, the explicit manifestation of eugenic and racial concerns has not been acceptable in academic discussion. Because a lot is left unsaid, comprehending the real meaning of the demographic agenda requires close scrutiny.

On the surface, the literature which discusses the relationship between population growth and Third World development appears free of the population fears associated with competitive fertility. Moreover, those who identify population growth as a major problem have self-consciously distanced themselves from the language of socio-biology. Teitelbaum and Winter have pointed to the shift from the racial theories to a more 'civilized discourse' in the forties (1985, p. 63). The change in vocabulary during the forties represented a major modification to the narrative of demography. Those involved in population studies were clearly compromised by the Nazi experiments with eugenics. As McNicoll remarked, the close relationship between professional demographers with eugenics, 'left demography severely embarrassed'.[16] After the Nazi experience, the language of demography became de-racialized. As one study of the relationship between American foreign and population policy noted 'World War II put an end to most public expressions of racist sentiments with respect to population control. Instead, attention shifted to anxiety over the impact of rapid growth of those who had not been properly socialized, whether they were a poor minority in an American urban area or the "Asiatic masses" (P. J. Donaldson, 1990, p. 20). The new vocabulary of demography clearly sought to distance itself from its previous flirtation with racial theory.

Many advocates of population control remain acutely conscious of the sensitive character of their enterprise. They are ever alert to the possibility that their motives could be interpreted as the pursuit of a geopolitical agenda. The anticipation of such accusations leads to the careful wording of demographic policies. Statements are painstakingly checked so that any reference to anxieties about competitive fertility is censored. Even allusions to the self-interest of the donor countries promoting population programmes are discouraged. As one advocate of population policy complained; 'what's rarely mentioned is that the promotion of lower fertility in the Third World is not only good for the recipients, but for the donor nations as well. That's us. The point is not made, however, because it is thought that it might sound colonial or racist'(Wattenberg, 1987, p. 161). Such concern with appearances means that the language of demography can only be fully understood if what is said is situated alongside the significant silences.

It is common for the very concern with population to be recycled in a masked form. Proponents of population control have discovered that, if their campaign is presented as a concern with health, it is possible to gain wider support for their project (see Symonds and Carder, 1973, p. 150). Consequently population control programmes are often made invisible through their integration into health services. Sometimes, advocates of family planning programmes claim that they are interested in issues that are far wider than the control of fertility. But as Warwick has noted, 'a close look' shows that 'in most cases, the heart of population policy is birth control and that other elements are introduced to diminish its prominence or not implemented' (Warwick, 1987, p. 31). The resources devoted to public relations in the field of population programmes suggests that this is an area where subterfuge and manipulation play an important role.

Another reason why the demographic debate cannot be understood in its own terms is that the identification of population growth as a problem is linked to broader social concerns. The focus on a 'population problem' is not a simple reaction to a specific demographic trend. Instead, the formulation of such a problem is the product of broad social currants and shifts in perception. As

Hodgson remarked, concern about population arises 'as much from value considerations as from demographic trends'.[17] Population issues are always intertwined with the major political and social problems of the time. Those who possess strong views on population problems are nevertheless pragmatic in how they express their sentiments. As the subsequent chapters indicate, the presentation of a population problem has gone through a number of distinct phases.

At the height of the Cold War, Western proponents of population control pointed to an alleged linkage between swelling numbers and the Communist threat. 'The major threat in Asia', wrote William Vogt back in 1949, 'is mounting population pressure in the Soviet Union' (Vogt, 1949, p. 238). During the next three decades, with the emergence of the Third World as a major influence in international affairs, the focus of population policy advocates shifted to the issue of development. Throughout this period population and development questions became entangled in public debate.

For a variety of reasons which are explored in subsequent chapters, the close association of population issues with that of development has been weakened. One important influence on this shift in emphasis has been the rise of environmental consciousness in the West. Popular interest in the environment has provided a hospitable intellectual setting for the promotion of population matters and those in the forefront of the population lobby have swiftly jumped on to the environmental bandwagon. The findings of Wilmoth and Ball's study of the population debate in American popular magazines is quite revealing in this respect. According to their survey, until the 1970s the arguments invoked about the dangers of population growth tended to stress issues like food shortages, the threat of famine and underdevelopment. By the eighties the dominant theme in published articles was the link between population growth and its destructive impact on the environment. Wilmoth and Ball concluded, that the 'most striking change' which occurred was 'in the estimated percent of articles citing the link between population and the environment, a link that goes from being a non-issue in 1946 to being the single most frequently invoked anti-growth argument in the 1980s'.[18]

The reorientation of demographic discourse from a developmental to an environmental vocabulary was influenced by the intellectual and political climate that prevailed in the West during the eighties. The more general questioning of the desirability of growth provided a new platform for advocates of population control. For many Neo-Malthusians, the growth of environmental consciousness came as an unexpected boost to their cause. As the author of a recently published Malthusian text, Virginia Abernethy, observed 'Most official environmental statements now indict population pressure as the root cause of stress. Increasingly, as well, the media pick up on the link between population size and the spreading environmental mess. This insight represents a sea change, one that seemed to get under way, in fact, while this book was in progress' (Abernethy, 1993, p. xiii). One of the ironies of the close association of demographic concerns with environmentalism, is that it now often indicts the developmental paradigm that was central to earlier advocates of population control.

The pragmatism with which leading population control enthusiasts dropped the programme of development and adopted environmentalism has remained a characteristic feature of the literature on this subject. Many reviews of the debate that took place at the 1994 Cairo Conference on population remarked on how women had become the central issue in the proceedings. 'The "empowerment of women" may not exactly trip off the tongue, but it has been constantly on the lips of government leaders and thousands of delegates and lobbyists during this nine-day event', observed one report on the Cairo Conference.[19] Today, gender has emerged as the dominant theme in the demographic discussion. It threatens to sideline – at least temporarily – the population–environment linkage.

The changing contours of demographic agenda are a testimony to the close relationship between the population issue and other, wider concerns. They also underline the pragmatism of many of those involved in the population field. The rationale for curbing population has changed many times. The shift from arguing that population growth threatens the economic well-being of Third World societies, towards pointing to the danger it represents to women's health, has involved a number of stops along the way. But while the arguments have changed, the conviction that population growth is 'the' problem has remained intact. The ability of the ideology of population control routinely to shed one explanation in favour of another, suggests that its apprehensions are independent of actual population trends. A cynic may also conclude that arguments about development or the environment are just that – arguments to justify a pre-existing concern with population growth. Certainly the apparent independence of the demographic obsession from any specific issue or event suggests that the fear of numbers needs to be understood in its own terms.

The independence of the preoccupation of demography from real trends in population growth is also reinforced by the tendency for concern with fertility to be motivated by non-demographic impulses. It is not merely a case of population anxieties looking for effective arguments. Sometimes debates that are far removed from demography are fought out on the battlefield of population. In recent years, for example, anti-immigrant sentiments have been represented through political arithmetic. The themes of population control in the Third World have become entangled with arguments about the urgency of containing the flow of immigrants to Europe and the United States.

The discussion on population has also been overwhelmed by controversies that are internal to the United States. During the Reagan–Bush era of the eighties, the influence of the New Right led to an important change of emphasis in American population policy. With the temporary ascendancy of free-market economics, the legitimacy of interventionist population programmes was called into question. This shift in emphasis became internationalized at the 1984 Conference on Population in Mexico, where the American delegates contended that population growth was a neutral phenomenon. Given the global influence of the United States, it was only a matter of time before international institutions such as the World Bank began to adopt a more neutral stance. This shift helped weaken the cause of population control. According to a supporter of such policies, it led to a 'dark mood of defeat and disarray within the international population community'.[20]

The impact of the American abortion debate on population discussions has also been far reaching. The American anti-choice lobby was able to influence the foreign population policy of the United States during the Reagan–Bush era. Since the eighties, conservative 'right to life' movements on both sides of the Atlantic have been active in the population debate. Religious activists, who lost the debate on the issue of a right of a women to abortion, have sought to relaunch the discussion on the international plane through their attacks on population control. Some of the most consistent attacks on neo-Malthusianism have come from this source. At times conservative organizations like the Society for the Protection of Unborn Children (SPUC) adopt a radical, even anti-imperialist vocabulary in their literature. A SPUC review of the Cairo Conference attacked those who want to `rid the earth of millions of babies supposedly to improve the environment or the economy'. The author of the review remarked, that 'these fanatics give the words "master race" a new meaning.'[21]

The clash between those who support a women's right to abortion and those who oppose it clearly impinged on the proceedings at the Cairo and the Beijing conferences. More than ever before, a discussion ostensibly about demographic matters provided an opportunity for a clash of views about values, traditions and acceptable forms of sexual behaviour. Western debates about abortion and family values became inextricably bound up with the debate about population growth in the South.

The convergence of Western domestic debates about moral values with controversies regarding international population trends ensured that the proceedings at Cairo received an unprecedented degree of media publicity. But the general interest in population matters goes way beyond the manoeuvres at a conference. As humanity moves towards the twenty-first century, demographic consciousness has acquired a new intensity in Western societies. Extravagant language is deployed to represent the Third World as one big population problem. The general mood that prevails is one of a heightened sense of limits. The failure of social experimentation together with a disenchantment with modernity has strengthened scepticism towards belief in progress. Developments in social theory reflect this pessimism. The term 'Risk Society' well captures the sentiment of foreboding towards the future. This *fin-de-siècle* malaise directly questions the ability of people to deal with the problems that lie ahead. In this context, the fear of the consequences of population growth influences virtually the entire spec-

---

CHANGING RATIONALE FOR POPULATION POLICY

During the past three decades, one rationale for population policy has given way to another. Traditionally population policy was justified on the ground that it would help remove the main obstacle to economic development.

Since the late seventies economic arguments in favour of population control have given way to other justifications. These are:

● The need to protect the environment
● The need to empower women
● The need to curb global migration
● The need to defend international stability

trum of social thought. It is not just pessimistic conservatives but also chastened self-acclaimed Marxists who share a strong consciousness of limits.[22]

The range of problems attributed to population growth continues to change and expand.Yet there is always another agenda at work behind the numbers game. At this point it is well worth considering the question: does population growth really matter?

2

Does Population Growth Matter?

The numerical growth in the world's population has been truly impressive. In 1960, there were around 3 billion people in the world. Since then, world population has almost doubled to around 5.7 billion. The Department for Economic and Social Information and Policy Analysis at the United Nations Secretariat has provided long-range projections of the world's population. According to the three variants used – 'low', 'medium' and 'high' rates of fertility – world population in 2025 will be 7.5, 8.5 or 9.4 billion (United Nations, 1994, pp. 211–12). Most of this future growth is accounted for by projected population increases in the world's poorer regions in Africa, Asia and Latin America. But what significance should be attached to these projections? Does rapid population growth really matter? And is it a threat to human or social welfare?

Fast rates of population growth are a relatively recent development. Throughout most of human history, the world was inhabited by relatively few people. The numbers of people tended to be fairly static because the prevailing forms of social organization and production techniques limited the amount of available food. This was the norm in many prehistoric societies. With the introduction of settled agriculture, food production rose and world population gradually increased. However, the phenomenon of rapid population growth dates only from the development of industrial societies and their global expansion in the eighteenth and nineteenth centuries. A fast-rising rate of population growth was clearly bound up with the rise of industrial capitalism and so was most marked in nineteenth-century Europe and North America. The rapid increase in the rate of population growth was primarily a consequence of the fall in the death rate during the nineteenth century.

As a result of the experience of industrialization, fast rates of population growth were often associated with economic dynamism and prosperity. The increase in numbers was welcomed as a contribution to fulfilling the need for an expanded workforce and to stimulating the expansion of the market. At the time, most experts regarded population growth as a positive by-product of industrial development. Consequently, when the rate of fertility first began to fall in Western industrial societies, the general response was one of concern.

In the twentieth century, perceptions about the consequences of rapid population growth have been more ambiguous than in the past. One reason for this change of attitude is that rapid population growth has no longer been linked to economic dynamism and industrial development. Instead, the geographical locus of population growth has shifted to the less developed parts of the world. The growth of population during this century, in Africa, Asia and Latin America, has had little to do with any dynamic socio-economic process. This growth in population can be interpreted as an unintended consequence of the global expansion of western influence. It was the introduction of basic public health measures in African, Asian and Latin American societies, and not economic dynamism, which contributed most to the fall of the death rate. So in the South, substantial increases in population have occurred without the socio-economic changes that accompanied population growth in the Western European experience.

The link between a fast rate of population growth and economic dynamism has also been ruptured by the tendency towards falling rates of fertility in developed societies. Both the United States and Europe have experienced a decline in fertility. The stabilization of population size within these more prosperous developed societies, alongside high rates of population growth in the less prosperous developing world, has helped to consolidate negative perceptions of rapid population growth. In the late twentieth century, population growth tends to be equated with famine and poverty, while rising living standards are associated with low rates of fertility and small families.

At any given time, perceptions about the impact of demographic trends are shaped by the prevailing patterns of social and economic life. In the nineteenth century, population growth was linked to economic success. This view continued to influence policy-makers well into this century. For example during the Great Depression of the 1930s, many influential thinkers associated economic stagnation with static rates of population growth. In Britain, calls for the setting up of a Royal Commission on Population were motivated by the fear that future prosperity depended on an increase in the rate of fertility. As late as the thirties poverty was seen as the outcome of a slow rate of population growth, whereas today it is seen as the consequence of a rapid rate of growth. This diametrically opposite conclusion is drawn, because today there seems to be an inverse relationship between per capita living standards and population growth.

Since so many different consequences have been attributed to population growth, its very status as a causal factor in economic trends remains unclear. Who is right? Those who argued in the past that economic stagnation was the consequence of slow growth of population, or those who contend today that a high rate of population growth leads to poverty? Among the specialists, there is no consensus on the links between population and economic performance, either in the thirties or today. This debate is not helped by a tendency to try to explain too much. The divergent experiences indicate that there is no simple relation of causality at work. What we do know for certain is that in the thirties there was an economic depression and that this coincided with a slow-down in population growth. But the coincidence of these two phenomena may well be just that – a coincidence. We also know that today there is a coincidence between high rates of population growth and widespread poverty. Again, the coincidence of these factors does not necessarily imply a causal relationship between the two.

At any time in history, developments in economic or social life obviously coincide with the prevailing rate of population growth. But whether these are either directly or indirectly influenced by demographic trends is far from self-evident.

2.1 What Kind of a Relationship?

Most serious contributions to the debate on demographic issues acknowledge that there is no direct relationship between population growth and specific social and economic trends. However, such a concession about the 'complexity' of the relationship in no way diminishes the significance attached to it by proponents of demographic consciousness. An *a priori* belief in the significance of demography coexists with an apparent theoretical openness about the nature of the relationship. That this theoretical openness is only superficial is demonstrated by the terms within which concessions about the 'complexity' of the problem are presented. Take the UN's *World Economic and Social Survey 1994* as an example.

> Although it is important to identify the interrelationships between population and socio-economic variables, their complexity makes it difficult to identify the exact causal factors at work and to assess the stability of the interrelationships that are observed at one particular time or in a particular setting. The analysis of the relationship between population and socio-economic development is necessarily highly specific, but the issues themselves are of critical importance to the international community (1994, p. 208).

Here, a timely affirmation of the specificity of the relationship between population and social trends is directly contradicted by the *a priori* generalization about its 'critical importance'. How does the author of the report know that a link is important before the work of analysis has been completed? In this example, analysis and explanation are deemed external to a discourse that is somehow self-evidently critically important. Something that is taken to be highly specific in one breath is prejudged in another.

The specialist literature exhibits a profound tension between the intuition that population growth has negative consequences for the living standards of developing societies, and the absence of empirical evidence to substantiate this sentiment. Two supporters of population policy conceded recently that, when it comes to deciding on the impact of population growth, 'feelings' still tend to count for more than facts: 'The contradictions in the mind of Malthus still confront many analysts and policymakers in the population field, those whose feelings, impressions, and personal certainties about the negative effects of population growth are not supported by a careful sifting of the facts.'[1] The admission that intuition and sentiment continue to drive the discussion on population growth should raise some important questions about the direction the debate is taking.

The sentiment which attaches critical importance to population growth is predicated on some variant of the Malthusian model. Such models uphold a thesis which posits a direct relation between population and social trends. In one form or another, the model is constructed on a foundation where most of the key factors other than the rate of growth of population are assumed to be more or less fixed. According to this scenario, the earth has a fixed or limited 'carrying capacity', it contains fixed resources, and there is a fixed amount of land available for the production of food. Since more or less everything else is fixed, the rate of population growth becomes the key variable. From this assumption, it follows that increases in the rate of population growth can only lead to a reduction in the availability of resources. From the standpoint of demographic consciousness, people are primarily consumers rather then producers. The contribution that people can potentially make to improve, enhance and develop the quality of life of their communities is left out of the equation. People are seen as so many mouths that need to be fed rather than new pairs of hands that can produce more food. People are also represented more as problems rather than problem-solvers.

From time to time, in retrospect, advocates of population policy will concede that people have creatively overcome some Malthusian trap. They will acknowledge that a particular method of production or technology has been instrumental in overcoming the previously anticipated limits. However, such experiences are generally presented as one-off or temporary interventions. According to the model, human technical progress is but a temporary trend, whereas the reality of limited resources and the law of diminishing returns possess a universal historical significance. A recent report published by the Population Action International exemplifies this approach. While it recognizes that human ingenuity has led to consistent increases in agricultural output, it warns that 'we also know that the world is now feeding itself using techniques that will not maintain natural resources over long time periods.' It notes that agricultural research is likely to produce other high-yield crop strains in the future, yet concludes on the ominous note that this 'may merely hold the line against the spread of malnutrition' (Engelman and Roy, 1995, pp. 7, 24). Throughout the report, human innovation is depicted as a transitory palliative to a universal iron law of diminishing returns.

In fact, both historical and contemporary experience suggest that social trends cannot be explained by reference to the size of a population or its relation to 'natural' resources. How people live and at what standard of living is not directly related to population density. Nor does the standard of living of people depend on the amount of land or resources available to them. There are many prosperous societies from Singapore to Iceland, which enjoy economic success regardless of a dearth of important physical resources. Just as poverty is not the necessary outcome of a lack of resources, so too wealth is not the automatic consequence of natural abundance. The prevalence of poverty in resource-rich societies, from Brazil to Nigeria, indicates that living standards are not the direct product of nature. Indeed in some societies, the most important resource is seen to be people. Singapore actually reversed its population control policies in the 1980s when it realized that they were jeopardizing its main economic resource – its skilled labour force (see Drakakis-Smith, 1992, p. 102).

From the available evidence, the only safe conclusion that can be drawn is that the relationship between population and resources or population and living standards is indeterminate. This indeterminacy is not surprising, since closer inspection suggests that the meanings of 'population' and 'resources' are themselves far from clear. Let us look at both terms more closely.

There can be very little gain in understanding if population is treated as a simple quantitative phenomenon. The nature of societies cannot be grasped as the consequence of crude numbers. What is a population? The number of people living within the confines of a given territory? In reality people are not numbers. They exist in communities which are governed by a diverse range of cultural, economic and social influences. As a result of these influences people adapt to their circumstances in different ways. People do not relate to natural resources directly, but through their institutions and social organization and with different levels of technology.

Communities tend to face crises such as endemic poverty or famine, not because of their numbers, but because of their relative lack of control over their circumstances. Nineteenth-century Ireland provides the classic example of the indeterminate relationship between numbers and living standards. The population of Ireland fell from over 8 million in 1840 to 4,260,000 in 1940 according to the French demographer Alfred Sauvy (1969, p. 273). Back in the early nineteenth century the poverty of Ireland was blamed on its overpopulation. The 2 million people who starved to death within ten years of the onset of the potato famine of 1846 were presented as victims of some Malthusian trap. In reality the problem was very different. Throughout the famine, vast amounts of food continued to be shipped to Britain. It was Ireland's colonial status rather then its rate of fertility which bore a large share of the blame for this tragedy. The experience of Ireland also demonstrates the fact that even a steady fall in population does not produce economic or social benefits. As the number of Irish peasants was drastically reduced, poverty persisted.

How communities cope with their circumstances cannot be deduced from an inspection of population densities. While Irish peasants starved and were forced to migrate, their counterparts in late nineteenth-century Japan were participants in a momentous process of social and economic development. The different trajectories of these two populations suggests the irrelevance of numbers and the importance of social organization, political institutions and technology.

The term population, on its own, has little more then a quantitative significance. The other side of the Malthusian equation, that of resources, is also less than self-evident. Nothing is in and of itself a resource. It is through the interaction of societies with nature that things can become considered as resources. Throughout most of human history the oceans were conceived of as an obstacle that limited people's activity. They were depicted more as a problem than a resource. At a certain point of social and technological development, however, what was regarded as an obstacle came to be seen as a means for travel. Today, the oceans are considered to be a treasure-house of resources. Similarly for most societies, throughout history, neither uranium nor bauxite was a resource. They became sought-after minerals through development and human experience. Other minerals, such as coal, which were highly prized in the past, are today no longer considered to be a particularly valuable resource. The closure of coal mines throughout Europe indicates the fluid relationship between people and resources.

Resources, like people, have a history. Different materials and sources of energy acquire the character of a resource through the historical interaction between human societies and nature. That is why it is confusing to discuss the term 'resources' as if it were a pre-given quantity that we know and whose quality we understand. Resources, like population, acquire a meaning in specific social and historical contexts. It is this social context which mediates the relationship between people and nature. From this perspective, the contemporary phenomenon described as `pressure on resources' can be understood not so much as the consequence of numbers but of the failure of society to adapt. That is why in many situations, if the failed institutions and methods are retained, a reduction in population does not have any positive effect on the quality of life. Contemporary Russia, where a fall in the rate of fertility has been matched by a stagnation of living standards, illustrates this point.

Many rural societies, which have experienced a fall in population density due to out-migration, have nonetheless failed to improve their agricultural production. The depopulation of Gascony in nineteenth century France, for example, did not bring about an increase in agricultural productivity (United Nations, 1953, p. 271). In some cases the migration of rural cultivators actually made the situation worse. In parts of Nepal, it was the depopulation of the mountainsides through migration which led to major environmental problems. With the reduction of the population, there were simply not enough people to manage and maintain the agricultural terraces, replant trees and 'carry on the practices that have sustained mountain agriculture for thousands of years'.[2] In this case, a fall in population indirectly resulted not in an increase but a decrease of available resources. It would be wrong, however, to conclude from the Nepalese experience that a loss of population inevitably has negative consequences for resource management or for the quality of life. In some societies, the reduction of the rural population would not have any adverse effect. Societies working with different technologies and under different forms of community organization can adapt to and minimize the consequences of a loss of population.

The key point here is that, in itself, an increase or decrease in population determines nothing. Facts which inform us about the changing level of population can, on their own, explain very little. Indeed it is the loss or increase in population that needs to be explained. Demographic changes occur within a wide framework of social development and their significance cannot be determined in isolation from these factors.

2.2 The Isolation Effect

Population statistics on their own reveal very little of significance. Figures can be produced to demonstrate the phenomenal rise of population this century. But figures can also be used to show the phenomenal growth of life expectancy, technological change or energy consumption over the same period. Indeed everything seems to have grown 'phenomenally' this century. The so-called population explosion looks far less significant when set alongside the explosion of air travel or food production. Statistical increases do not speak for themselves. Nor is it clear what consequences if any arise from numerical growth. For example in the United Kingdom, private car licenses have increased by more than 2,000 per cent this century. This period has also coincided with Britain's relative decline as a great power. To draw a link between the rise of vehicle licences and Britain's decline would be no more forced than to suggest a direct connection between population statistics and living standards.

Interpretations based on crude numbers tend to be arbitrary, since in reality human beings cope differentially according to their social arrangements. Terms like overcrowding and overpopulation are value judgements that often masquerade as facts. Over two thousand years ago, wealthy aristocrats were building villas in the countryside surrounding Rome on the grounds that the city was overcrowded. 'Overcrowded' cities would not be cities if they had the population densities characteristic of rural areas. Ironically many young people cannot wait to leave their towns of origin for the big overcrowded cities. Others renounce the same urban condition because they consider it inconsistent with healthy living.

Paul Ehrlich's reaction to an evening out on the town with his wife and daughter in Delhi helps explain this subjective sense of overpopulation:

> The streets seemed alive with people. People eating, people washing, people sleeping. People visiting, arguing, screaming. People thrusting their hands through the taxi window, begging. People defecating and urinating. People clinging to buses. People herding animals. People, people, people, people. As we moved slowly, through the mob, hand horn squawking, the dust, noise, heat, and cooking fires gave the scene a hellish aspect. Would we ever get to our hotel? All three of us were, frankly, frightened . . . Old India hands will laugh at our reaction. We were just some overprivileged tourists, unaccustomed to the sights and sounds of India. Perhaps but since that night I've known the feel of overpopulation' (1971, p. 1).

Ehrlich's term, the 'feel of overpopulation' is curiously apposite, for above all his reaction is an expression of a feeling. It is this subjective reaction that leads affluent people to leave overcrowded London or New York for the more spacious suburbs. And yet, from Ehrlich's portrayal of Delhi, it is possible to draw a very different conclusion: that on that fateful evening, what he saw was the effects of a lack of housing and sanitation facilities, and poverty.

Moreover, what he feared was not just people as such, but human beings who were desperately poor and living on the edge.

A concept like population growth begs more questions than it provides answers. Its consequences are inseparable from the influences that continue to shape the patterns of fertility. Population growth in the context of widespread urbanization has different implications and trajectory than it would among, say, a nomadic community. Calculations about fertility are subject to a variety of historical and social influences. The social process through which people exist and interact with nature have only an external existence in the Malthusian world view. From the standpoint of demographic consciousness, the rate of growth of population in and of itself exercises a decisive influence. That is why, when he was in India, Ehrlich could see only 'people, people, people, people'. This reaction was predicated on the pre-existing conviction that imagines population growth as the dominant force shaping societies. As Ester Boserup wrote in relation to the Malthusian world view 'population growth is here regarded as the independent variable which in its turn is a major factor determining agricultural developments' (1993, p. 11).

One of the central methodological failings of the Malthusian literature is its isolation of population from both history and social development. The most consistent Malthusians portray population as an independent variable, that is driven by its own laws and in isolation from wider social forces. Yet, although there is no consensus on the relationship between population growth and the wider patterns of social development, most studies suggest that the two are inseparable from one another. Decisions about fertility are influenced by expectations of the future. Urbanization and industrialization are usually – though not always – linked to the reduction in family size. Standards of living, health and education are also crucial influences on the rate of fertility of any society.

The isolation of population from socio-historical change provides the intellectual underpinning of population policy. The scope for the pursuit of population policies would be far more limited if demographic trends were located within a wider socio-cultural setting. The Chinese example indicates that this setting cannot be ignored. The single-minded ruthless pursuit of a 'one-child' policy in China has certainly curbed the rate of growth of fertility. However, it is interesting to note that Chinese population policy was far more successful in the urban than in the rural areas. The nature of employment and welfare in the urban setting reduced the need for children – even for sons. The absence of this socio-economic context in rural China has meant that attitudes to fertility are far more resistant to change than in the cities.[3] For example in a large city like Shanghai, the annual birth rate is 10.3 per thousand, comparable to that of Italy and less than that of the United States. In contrast in rural Xiajiang, the birth rate is that of 26.4 per thousand, similar to that of Surinam or Panama.[4]

Isolating the population variable provides a methodological justification for the implementation of population policies. The most committed advocates of population control argue that the rate of fertility can be changed, preferably reduced, regardless of the wider patterns of development. From this standpoint, the attempt to associate changes in the rate of fertility with a wider pattern of social development makes little sense. This is the argument advanced by Robey, Rutstein and Morris, who minimize the importance of the wider picture. They concede that development helps encourage small family size, but argue that population policies can work regardless of social change since 'contraceptives are the best contraceptives.'[5] This conclusion, that population policies are effective regardless of the circumstances, has become influential in recent years. Livi-Bacci has even suggested that 'where development is sluggish, population policies have an autonomous important role, and by bringing down fertility they may accelerate development.'[6] This analysis based on the autonomous role of population growth, and of policies designed to combat its effect, leads to a model where demography exists in a compartment that is isolated from the rest of the world.

Bangladesh is often used to illustrate the argument that demographic trends can be modified regardless of the wider patterns of development. Norman Myers boasted that although Bangladesh is 'one of the poorest countries on Earth' the usage of contraception doubled in the eighties; 'offering further reason to believe that sheer socio-economic advance is not an invariable prerequisite for further fertility decline'.[7] It is far from clear whether population policies alone accounted for the decline of fertility in Bangladesh.[8] That the single-minded pursuit of population control can have an effect on the rate of fertility is beyond doubt, but whether such policies have any consequences for the quality of life is far from clear. The absence of any amelioration in living standards in Bangladesh seems to suggest the implementation of population policies may not result in any social or economic benefits. Contraceptives can prevent the birth of babies, but they do not increase output of food or the quality of life.

The widespread use of the Bangladeshi example confirms that population control rather than social and economic progress is the point of the contemporary argument. This case is meant to demonstrate the irrelevance of socio-economic processes and to highlight the efficacy of population policy. But efficacy to what end? Why is population control important in its own terms? For Myers and his co-thinkers, population growth matters not because of its effect on social welfare but because they believe that more people are intrinsically problematic.

The isolation of the population variable leads to a form of analysis which tends to endow demographic trends with their own inner drive. Sometimes, treating population as an autonomous force even leads to the conclusion that there is an independent culture of fertility in particular societies. The high rates of population growth in Africa in particular have been explained as the result of a peculiar African culture of fertility. Some writers suggest that in Africa, cultural traditions and particularly the attitudes of men towards work, help consolidate a regime of high fertility. 'Unlike many traditional societies those in sub-Saharan Africa generally had no concept of having enough children' wrote two of the most well known authorities on the subject.[9] As Sherrif Sonko observed, 'it is the contention here that the reasons for persistently high fertility in sub-Saharan Africa are cultural.'[10]

Culture no doubt influences decisions about fertility. But culture, like other products of human experience, is not immutable. The argument of John and Pat Caldwell, two leading demographers specializing in Africa, that fertility practices are based on a culture going back hundreds of years is strikingly ahistorical.[11] Theories of African exceptionalism one-sidedly abstract demography from the wider set of social relations and reduce its causes to the workings of a unique tradition of high fertility. It is unlikely that such a special tradition of fertility could have evolved on its own, without interacting with other aspects of historical development. Regimes of high fertility generally represent a response to specific social conditions such as high rates of mortality. But to even posit a distinctive 'African culture of fertility' requires an indifference to the rich variations in traditions within that continent. Jewsiewicki has noted, for example how among the Zulu, 'having children was not always a dominant social value'.[12]

The lack of validity for the thesis of an African culture of high fertility is demonstrated by the interwar consensus that prevailed among demographers. This suggested that the problem facing the continent was that of 'underpopulation' and low rates of fertility. Most of the early studies of African demography warned about the danger facing societies which could barely replace their numbers. Kuczynski's three-volume magisterial study, *Demographic Survey of the British Colonial Empire* (1948), continually refers to such warnings. For example, the prominent British imperial official, Sir Fredrick Lugard is cited in 1900 as stating that since the arrival of colonialism in Africa 'the native populations in most territories have not increased and have probably decreased' (p. 48). It is astonishing that today's literature, which advocates the thesis of the African culture of high fertility makes such little use of historical sources.

High rates of population growth in Africa have evolved in the context of a complex of socio-economic and cultural development. There can be little doubt that in many parts of the continent, the desire for large families is underwritten by custom and a variety of cultural practices, but such customs and traditions are far from eternal or resistant to modification. As in other societies, they are fluid and subject to change. The persistence of some of these customs alongside high rates of population growth can best be understood as the product of the limited pattern of socio-economic development in Africa. Throughout most parts of the world, fertility decline was the outcome of industrialization and the changes that accompanied this process. Such changes have evolved only to a limited extent in most parts of Africa. One of the most important of these changes is the consistent increase in the share of the population involved in occupations which are conducive to small family size. These are mainly occupations which are located in the urban areas and require higher education – occupations which are relatively rare in most parts of Africa. Boserup also pointed to the significance of another change which has helped to reduce family size elsewhere: the declining importance of child labour in circumstances where 'land reforms provide security through land ownership, and as sources of non familial support in old age and emergencies develop'. She concluded;

> In most of Africa, this process has barely begun. The level of industri-
> alisation and urbanisation is still low, and agricultural technology is
> primitive. Furthermore, special features of African land tenure and
> family organisation encourage high fertility. These factors are also
> related to the delayed economic development that explains the preser-

vation of cultural features that have disappeared in most other parts of the world.[13]

So according to Boserup, it is not an autonomous African culture of fertility that explains the prevailing demographic trends. The high rates of population growth are the outcome of a form of one-sided development, where industrialization, the creation of formal urban employment and the establishment of land reform have evolved slowly and unevenly. For example, Africa has the lowest proportion of population living in urban areas. Under these cir-cumstances, the forces that have influenced changes in attitudes towards family size in other countries, are still conspicuously weak.

The attempt to isolate a particular African culture of fertility is all the more surprising since the link between population growth and prevailing economic problems is highly tenuous. Africa is the only continent which has failed to raise per capita agricultural output in the past thirty years. However, it is difficult to imagine that population growth bears any responsibility for the crisis of African agriculture. As the Report of the National Research Council noted, 'Africa has a relatively high ratio of arable land to population, which suggests that the decline in per capita agricultural output reflects factors other than diminishing returns due to population growth' (1986).

The tendency to isolate demographic trends is by no means restricted to those who advocate population policies. Many writers appear to get carried away by their subject and devotedly search for what they characterize as 'population induced changes'. Such a term contains major difficulties. In any situation, it is difficult to indicate which of the changes under consideration were induced by population growth. For example, new forms of agricultural practices can be a response to population growth but also to the availability of new technology, changing market conditions, im-provements in infrastructure, even shifts in the world economy. As noted previously the coincidence of change with a particular demographic trend need not imply a causal relation. And yet, this is precisely the conclusion drawn by the editors of a series of African case studies. They argue that 'the autonomy of the demo-graphic variables should be taken seriously' since 'population as much as – if not more than – economy seems to drive what is happening there' (Turner, Hyden and Kates, 1993, pp. 432–3).

Some of the key pro-natalist writers on the subject share the tendency to isolate population. So someone like Julian Simon, who is a strident critic of the Malthusian perspective, implicitly accepts the methodological premise of his opponents. Simon offers a convincing critique of anti-natalist ideas. However, his criticisms are primarily directed against the association of population growth with negative consequences. He accepts the methodological isolation of fertility, though the conclusions he draws are diametrically opposed to the Malthusian perspective. To his credit, Simon is careful not to reduce demographic causality to one single relation. He notes that any 'model of population that concludes that any one fertility structure is unconditionally better or worse than another must be wrong' since it is too simplistic. So in this sense, his theory is far more specific and contextual than most contributions on the subject. But at the same time, he puts forward an analysis which assumes that population growth has direct economic consequences. For example, he wrote that in some circumstances 'extremely high fertility offers the highest income per capita and output per worker in the long run' (Simon, 1981, p. 281).

The assumption of direct connections between fertility and economic performance is evident in Simon's association of regimes of low fertility with poor economic performance. For Simon, low rates of fertility are a problem because of a tendency to narrow total demand in the market. This thesis, which was fashionable amongst underconsumptionist economists in the interwar period, logically leads to support for pro-natalist population policies: the more people, the bigger the market, the more growth. In many respects they are the mirror-image of the Malthusian contributors. So for Simon, in so far as there is a 'population trap', it is the opposite to that suggested by Malthus. Simon argues that the real problem occurs when 'population growth declines too fast'. The result of such decline is a fall in investment and income (1981, p. 281).

In Simon's case, the consequences of methodologically isolating population are minimal. Indeed his methodological isolationism is far from consistent. In places he recognizes that 'there is no simple relationship' between population and economic growth (1981, p. 285). Others have gone a step further, and have sought to isolate a 'Boserup-effect', that is to abstract the impact of population-induced changes. For example, on the basis of this isolation exercise, Evenson has concluded that 'there are indeed significant population-induced or Boserup effects in northern India.'[14] In practice, it is difficult to pinpoint actions that can clearly be defined as the outcome of population growth. The effect of larger numbers of people on social conditions is not self-evident. Prevailing forms of social organization absorb people differentially. In the realm of economic calculation, population is only one of a number of variables that influence decisions.

2.3 Isolating the Individual

The methodology of treating demography as an independent phenomenon leads the population lobby to a highly individualistic orientation. If the rate of fertility can be meaningfully discussed in isolation from wider macroprocesses, then the main site of demographic interest becomes that of individual behaviour and decision-making. Consequently, in much of the recent population literature, the focus is on individual attitudes towards fertility. Terms like 'fertility preference' are used to convey the element of individual motivation. They assume that decisions about family size are not so much the outcome of prevailing social circumstances, but of individual preference. Leading advocates of population control portray the subjective inclinations of individuals as the main influence behind high rates of fertility. John Bongaarts, the director of the Research Division of the Population Council has suggested that 'preferences for high fertility remain one of the fundamental causes of high birth rates and rapid population growth'.[29]

In one sense, the focus on individual preference is even inconsistent with some aspects of the previously discussed methodology of abstracting demography from its social context. At least the concept of a culture of fertility recognized that there was a complex of traditions and legacies which shaped decisions about family size. With the more individualistic emphasis, choices about fertility are situated even outside the context of culture. The practical consequences of this theoretical orientation are population policies which target individual attitudes towards fertility and seek to shape individual preference.

The individualistic focus of the population lobby is clearly expressed in the term 'unmet need'. The term suggests that there is a vast demand for contraception on the part of Third World women, which at the moment is unmet. The scope of this unmet need has not been empirically substantiated, but that does not inhibit publications from claiming that one in four births in the

developing world is unwanted. Some publications offer as proof
the argument that there are millions of abortions in the Third
World. Some reports claim the figure of 25 million such abortions
per year, others inflate the figure to 50 million. These speculative
figures are put forward as hard evidence to clinch the case for
population policies. There can be little doubt that many women in
developing societies want and need safe contraception, but the
absence of such facilities cannot explain the prevailing rates of
fertility. A study by Bongaarts and his colleague, Judith Bruce,
pointed out that the length of distance to family planning facilities
was not a particularly decisive factor in contraceptive prevalence.[16]

In the past, societies have been able to control their fertility
without access to modern forms of contraception. There is no
evidence which suggests that women in developing societies are
less able to control their fertility than their sisters in the past in other
parts of the world. According to the anthropologist Arthur Tuden,
among the Ila people of Zambia, a regime of low birth rate was
maintained since 'offspring were not highly desired by women'.
Through a combination of birth control practices – infanticide,
abortion and a two-and-a-half year post parturition taboo restrict-
ing intercourse – a very low rate of birth prevailed (cited in T.
Johnson, 1995, p. 16).

The concept of unmet need can only be upheld by abstracting
individuals from their social and cultural existence. It generalizes
from the experience of societies where the norm of a small family
regime has created 'unwanted children', to those where large
numbers of offspring are seen as essential for survival. Riedmann's
critique of this approach stresses how differently children are
regarded in Africa from in the West. For example survey questions
about 'your own children' make little sense in a situation where
they belong as much to the lineage as to a particular mother
(Riedmann, 1993, p. 69). In this social milieu, the 'need' for children
can not be understood as a private decision between husband and
wife.

The lack of empirical evidence for the thesis of unmet need is
illustrated by the verbal acrobatics of those who try to justify the
arguments. According to the definition of the Population Council,
unmet needs can exist even when women are not aware of this
need. It argues that the key causes of unmet needs are: 'lack of
ready access to information or adequate fertility regulation services;
reluctance or inability to use contraception, even with knowledge
and access to services, because of concerns about potential side

effects of contraceptive methods or health issues; and spousal and other familial pressures'.[17] In other words, the Population Council can spot an unmet need, even if Third World women cannot. The spurious character of unmet need is implicitly recognized by population workers in the field. They would not have to rely on incentives, such as giving gifts to women, if there was a ready-made demand for their services.

Support for the unmet need approach has grown in recent years, since it provides a compelling rationale for population control. The identification of a need represents an invitation for policy intervention. At the same time, the simplistic premise of the unmet need thesis has embarrassed the more rigorous Malthusians. For example, Paul Demeny, the editor of *Population and Development Review* has consistently opposed this focus. As he scathingly put it, the notion of unmet need implies that 'two billion people in the past 30 years were added to the world's population because their parents were too stupid to figure out what to do.'[18] Other studies have argued that research which promotes unmet need is deeply flawed.[19] Yet this thesis constitutes a central argument of the contemporary population lobby.

Criticisms of targeting the individual through the unmet need approach reveal the limits of the isolationist methodology. Most consistent Malthusians recognize that high rates of fertility are not due to a mistake. Most people end up with roughly the number of children that they actually need. Demographic surveys suggest that African women's 'ideal family size' ranges from six to nine children. According to the World Bank it is 'highly unlikely that provision of contraception alone will result in significant reductions in these figures' (Ainsworth, Beegle and Nyamele 1995, p. 1). That is why population policies are not designed to fulfil individual demand but to curb it. A hardline Malthusian, like Garrett Hardin, can argue that the freedom of individual families to breed should be subordinated to the needs of the common good. Hardin argues that left to their own instincts, individual families would breed without inhibitions.[20] The element of curbing the fertility preference of individual households is always implicit in the programme of population control.

2.4 Social policy and reproduction

The central argument of this chapter is that the relation between population growth and social welfare is indeterminate. The ideology of population control not only confuses the problems but also distracts attention from the real issues. Governmental support for population policies is based on the fact that in one sense there are always too many people relative to the amount of revenues it has at its disposal. Superficially it appears that if there were fewer people, more could be spent on each citizen. The problem of scarcity is one that every government encounters. Since it appears easier to reduce the population than to increase society's wealth and resources, many governments are drawn towards demographic solutions. That is why so many governments in the South are happy to accept resources from the West for the implementation of population policies.

It is evident that there often exists an imbalance between society and its ability to harness the potential of its people. The millions of unemployed, underemployed and impoverished are a testimony to this waste of human potential. However, this imbalance is not the consequence of rapid population growth but of the failure of social organization. The existence of millions of unemployed in Europe at a time when in many parts of the continent population growth is below replacement, is a testimony to the failure of social organization. Population policies in this context are clearly irrelevant to the situation. Instead of worrying about producing more children, effort could be more usefully deployed on working out policies designed to use the already living unemployed youth. At the other extreme is Africa. The coincidence of economic crisis and a high rate of population growth is just that – a coincidence. Africa has plenty of land to engage the energies of its people, what it lacks are the capital and effective political institutions to bring this about.

It could be argued that whatever the cause of Africa or any other developing region's problems, lowering the rate of population would at least make the situation better. There would be less pressure on resources and there would be more to go around for everyone. In the abstract it is true that a sudden reduction of the population would ease the immediate pressure on resources, but it would also lead to the reduction of output. Moreover a decrease in the size of the population would not solve any of the underlying problems. Inefficient institutions would not alter their character. Nor would a fall in population growth increase the amount of capital available to society. The benefits of population control in such circumstances would prove elusive.

Population policies – both anti- and pro-natal – are essentially an admission of the failure of existing social arrangements. It is difficult to imagine any circumstance where such a retreat to the realm of biological reproduction could advance the cause of social progress. The conclusion of this chapter is that demographic consciousness – the *a priori* disposition to interpret social problems through the prism of population – serves to distract attention from the fundamental socio-economic problems facing societies. In subsequent chapters, the experiences that have shaped the construction of demographic consciousness will be explored.

3

Population and North–South Relations

Pronouncements on population are rarely neutral statements about numbers. They are usually based on an agenda, which involves issues of resources, power and national interest. Demographic debates often express a clash of opinion about what constitutes the 'problem'. Those who talk about a population problem are often talking about the numbers of a people other than themselves. On the other side, reactions against proposals for controlling population tend to be most intense when the advocates of population control have a different ethnic or cultural background from those they seek to influence. This is particularly the case when population programmes are advocated by nations which have previously been seen as colonial oppressors. When the Zimbabwean MP Ruth Chinamano declared that campaigns designed to promote the use of contraception were a plot by developed nations to wipe out Africa, she expressed a view widely shared among opinion-makers in the developing world.

Doubts about the motives of Western advocates of population control are sometimes portrayed as the irrational reactions of Third World fundamentalists and dismissed as 'out of date' fears which have no basis in a 'post colonial world'. Instead, Western strategists and politicians today tend to justify their concern about demography as a response to the problems of poverty, the environment or women's health. However, the manner in which these authorities actually discuss Third World population suggests that their principal concern in fact has little to do with these issues. An examination of their literature reveals that the population agenda is strongly influenced by Western anxieties about its global position.

Of course, interest in demographic issues is by no means confined to the West. For example, the governments of Asian countries like China and India have their own perception of population problems. Although such perceptions need to be studied in their own right, they have been of little significance in setting the international population agenda. The West has played a central role in the problematization of demography as a global issue. From this standpoint, in the first instance, population growth is perceived as a problem for the West. Often this point is obscured by the fact that what is a problem for the West is ideologically represented as a threat to the welfare of the South. The aim of this chapter is to examine the main influences that helped shape the demographic consciousness which now prevails in the West.

Western demographic consciousness is strongly shaped by the consideration of strategic demography. The central focus of contemporary strategic demography is the contrast between falling birth rates in the North and rising birth rates in the South. In a lecture to the US Army conference on long-range planning in 1991, the American demographer Nicholas Eberstadt argued that if such a contrast continued for another generation or two, 'the implications for the international political order and the balance of world power could be enormous'. Pointing to a 'diminution' of the influence of the West, Eberstadt concluded that existing demographic trends 'could create an international environment even more menacing to the security prospects of the Western alliance than was the Cold War'[1]. This was also the thesis of Paul Kennedy's *Preparing For the Twenty-First Century* (1993), in which he argued that 'the relative diminution of their share of world population presents the industrial democracies with their greatest dilemma over the next thirty years' (p. 45).

Today's discussion on global demographic trends invariably counterposes an ageing, stagnant North to a vital and youthful South. The issue at stake is not just a massive demographic explosion in the South but also the loss of the reproductive impulse in the North. A leading contemporary French commentator, Pierre Lelouche has argued:

> the African population is projected to triple within the next 30 years, reaching an estimated level of 1.6 billion. Moreover, the Middle East, Central Asia and the Indian subcontinent all have volatile admixtures

of acute poverty, demographic explosion and political instability. Together these regions will have some 4 billion people within 30 years,
while due north sit 500 million ageing Europeans already in a squall of
demographic depression.[2]

A declining West with an ever-ageing population is portrayed as
a problem that is on a par with 'overpopulation' in the South. Both
developments become problems in relation to each other. The size
of a population is considered small or large, not in simple numerical terms, but relative to another.

Either implicitly or explicitly, studies of global demographic
trends assume that population has a considerable influence on
relations of power. Consequently, the relative increase in the
demographic weight of the Third World is experienced as a symptom of the decreasing global influence of the West. Since population is so directly linked to power, it has become an obvious subject
of comparison: demographic trends in one area are compared to
those of another. It is the changing relative population sizes that
dominate contemporary demographic debates. This theme is also
evident in the many ethnic, communal and religious conflicts that
afflict the societies of the South. Such demographic rivalry afflicts
societies like Nigeria, where the manipulation of census figures is
part and parcel of ethnic competition for controlling the resources
of central government.[3]

Concern about the relative change in population sizes between
North and South stems from an accepted belief that differences in
the rate of fertility have important implications for the distribution
of power. That is why the study of differential fertility has been an
important part of demographic research. It is widely believed that
numbers are important in settling competing claims on resources.
According to Wilson's *Dictionary of Demography*, differential fertility
often plays a major role in determining the relative socio-economic
and political status of different groups, especially those divided by
ethnic or religious status (Wilson, 1985, p. 186). The same assessment
of differential fertility informs global deliberations over the balance
of power.

According to the demographic perspective behind these deliberations, any change in population ratios must have important
implications for the outcome of global competition. Consequently,
the relative increase of the population of the South has long been
perceived as a potential source of geopolitical upheaval. A 1949
issue of UNESCO's *International Social Science Journal*, specially
devoted to the topic of 'International Tensions', pointed to

differential rates of population growth as a major cause for concern:

> The differential rate of growth, through varying degrees of control over the fertility and mortality of different continents, peoples, nations and communities, has, in a word , created the present world population problems which lead in some regions to starvation and disease, tension and wars. Whether population growth has now reached the demographic dangerspot of ultimate world explosion is a question which deserves to be examined.[4]

The conceptual link between differential population growth and war which was accepted at this time has continued to inform deliberations to this day.[5]

In fact, to identify 'overpopulation' or the 'population explosion' as 'the' problem is to confuse matters. The emphasis of the literature on differential fertility suggests that the cause of concern is not population growth in general, but a rise in numbers among particular ethnic groups. Whereas Malthus warned that human numbers generally would inevitably outstrip agricultural resources, it is now the power of 'their' population which is feared. Population control is usually advocated not merely for the control of numbers, but for numbers of a certain kind of people. Western governments, who preach the virtues of fertility control for the South, apply a different standard when it comes to their own societies. It is these contradictory attitudes of Western Governments towards demographic patterns in the North and in the South that inspires cynicism from many writers. Sumati Nair observed that the West German Government promoted population control in Bangladesh, but sought to counteract the effect of falling birth rate at home (Nair, 1989, p. 83). The policy of advocating more Germans and fewer Bangladeshis highlights the differential attitude to population growth.

Today, concerns about the impact of differential fertility on international relations are seldom expressed in crude balance of power terms. Western advocates of population control seldom mobilize explicit biological arguments about race and power, of a kind which would have been used in the past. Instead, the contemporary debate on differential fertility emphasizes its negative consequences for the survival of Western values. It is often argued that fertile Southern countries are precisely those whose governments reject democracy and individual rights. In this way, population increases in the South are represented as a danger to 'civilized values' rather than to a specific power bloc.[6] Sometimes, population control can even be represented as part of the West's humanitarian mission towards less fortunate societies. Bernard Kouchener, the founder of the well-known relief agency, Médecins Sans Frontiers, argued that 'world demographics need to be carefully monitored and a programme of sharing must be initiated', before pragmatically pointing to his principal concern – the danger of 'massive and uncontrollable immigration'.[7]

Since concern with differential fertility expresses fundamental conflicts of interests, the issues at stake are rarely expressed openly. There is a reluctance publicly to disclose fears regarding the outcome of demographic trends. Nevertheless, a glance at Western preoccupations with this subject indicates that the fear of losing global power is strong – and growing stronger too.

3.1 The Power of Numbers

The role of population for the determination of power is far from clear. Even military experts and strategists find it hard to establish a balance between numbers and security requirements.[8] In an era of high technology, strategic considerations are more about science and skills than they are about numbers.

The size of population was certainly an important factor in the past. In military conflicts, the number of soldiers fielded was frequently decisive. National power was clearly connected to the size of the population. For example many experts believed that the Franco–German rivalries of the nineteenth and twentieth centuries would be decided in the sphere of demography. Sections of the French elite argued that France's declining fertility was an evil which sapped the vitality of the nation. The attempt to implement strong pro-natalist policies by successive French governments reflected their fears for national survival. But France was not alone. Teitelbaum and Winter convincingly argue that throughout Europe the issue of national military defence was 'often expressed' in a 'demographic form'. They suggest, too, that European apprehensions of political and demographic decadence and decline were widespread during the period between 1870 and 1945 (1985, p. 17).[9]

Between the two world wars demography remained a fundamental component of international relations theory. It was acknowledged that European empires needed to confront the challenge of rising numbers of Asians. Western hegemony was often directly linked to the outcome of differential demographic patterns. A study commissioned by the Royal Institute of International Affairs, and written by Carr-Saunders, one of the world's leading demographers, was concerned with the question of how a relatively small number of people of European origin could continue to control most of the world. In America, Warren Thompson, one of the most influential demographers of the interwar period, was preoccupied with the same issue (see Carr-Saunders, 1936, and W. S. Thompson, 1929).

Western demographers were highly conscious of an anomaly whereby a relatively small number of Europeans monopolized most of the earth's real estate and resources. Pointing to the colonial empires, Carr-Saunders noted that Europeans were 'spread thinly'. He feared that the differential population growth in Europe and in the East would undermine the prevailing global distribution of power. 'This relatively light occupation of these overseas estates by their new master is one of the most important facts in the present state of world population', argued Carr-Saunders (1936, p. 45). That demographic patterns would prove decisive for the survival of the European empires was a view which the expert demographers effectively took as read.

The fear of the consequences of differential fertility continued to haunt Western policy-makers during and after the Second World War. As Peter Donaldson has shown, American policy-makers perceived rapid population growth in Asia as a threat to strategic interests (1990). Dudley Kirk spoke for American demography when he observed, in 1944, that differential population growth could alter the existing balance of power between the West and the East.[10] But the high rate of population growth in Asia was not just an anxiety of Americans but of British too. In Britain in 1946 a Royal Commission on Population pointed out that the decline of population in the West in relation to Asia 'might be decisive in its effects on the prestige and influence of the West'. It added: 'the question is not merely one of military strength and security: it merges into more fundamental issues of the maintenance and extension of Western views and culture' (see P. J. Donaldson, 1990, p. 18, and Symonds and Carder, 1973, p. 96).

In the literature of the time, the Pacific was often portrayed as the area where differential patterns of population growth could erupt in violent conflict. The 'empty spaces' of Australia were often contrasted to the overpopulated regions of Asia. One demographer speculated

> if Australia's population should cease to increase appreciably in the next ten years and if the population of Japan, China and India, and South-east Asia generally, should continue to grow as they have grown in the past half-century, the lack of balance between area and natural resources on the one hand and the population numbers on the other will lead sooner or later to some effort, violent or non-violent, to change the *status quo* in the Pacific and perhaps in the Americas.[11]

That there was a conflict of interest between thinly-populated European dominions and densely-inhabited regions of Asia was not in doubt. The question posed was how this conflict would be resolved in the period ahead.

In the context of North–South relations, differential population growth acquired a practical impact in the sphere of migration. It might be argued that, through the migration of Southerners to Northern regions, the world's population problems could be redistributed. However, many Western commentators interpreted the migration of people from the South as a violation of an already delicate balance of power. The titles of articles on the subject evoked powerful sentiments. Terms like 'danger' and 'peril' were typical. A 1923 paper by a leading American sociologist, 'The menace of migrating peoples', expressed the mainstream sentiment.[12] Whereas European expansion of the previous era was seen as a symptom of dynamism and vitality, migration, leading to a change in the distribution of the world's population, was seen as a symptom of Western decline, along with the falling rate of fertility of Western societies.

The question of migration brought and continues to bring Northern fears about Southern population growth to the surface. Most Western commentators on this issue have demanded controls on Southern migration. Such controls on the movement of people are justified on the grounds that immigrants are culturally or racially different from people of European origin. Behind the debate about numbers lurk other motifs. In the course of discussing global migration, demographers and other specialists reveal that their concern is not population as such, but the growth of certain types of population. All the literature suggests that problems are seen not merely as, quantitative, but qualitative. Contributions on the quality of population stress intelligence, health and other biological characteristics. Discussions of 'Australia's Population Problem', self-consciously emphasized that 'coloured' migration was not the answer to this country's need for a larger population.[13] Thus, immigration controls are advocated in order to keep out the wrong kind of people.

Carr-Saunders himself wanted restricted migration on the grounds that certain people could not easily be assimilated by a host society: 'The exclusion of non-Europeans from European countries overseas is probably wise because the very different traditions of non-Europeans possibly expressing genetic temperamental differences, are likely to be very persistent owing to physical differentiation which makes it unlikely that the process of assimilation can be satisfactorily accomplished' (1936, p. 219). Other demographers expressed similar reservations on the quality of the population of the South. Their hostility to immigration had varied roots: cultural, biological, racial. 'The potential migrants are in the main illiterate rural peasantry with very limited, if any, industrial training and skills' wrote one American contributor in 1956, only to continue that the 'potential emigrants are largely "yellows", "blacks" and "browns"; the people of the target areas mainly "whites"' (Hertzler, 1956, pp. 222–3).

Objections to the 'quality' of migrants from the South was not confined to a handful of eccentric or marginal specialists. This was, and continues to be, the dominant approach on the subject. The strong feelings and emotions provoked by the subject often indicate an absence of scholarly detachment. Thus Sir Julian Huxley, a former Director of UNESCO and a world-renowned scientist, compared the movement of people from the South to the North to the growth of a disease. Pointing, in 1963, to immigration into Britain and the USA from the Caribbean, he argued;

> It is comparable to what happens in human cancers, where unlimited multiplication produces what are called metastases – groups of cells that migrate to another part of the body and start trouble there. I would say that it is perfectly legitimate to compare the invasions of Puerto Ricans in New York and of Jamaicans in London and other parts of Britain to metastases in cancer. They are causing considerable social difficulties in their new homes – not primarily because of race prejudice, but because groups of people with different habits and different standards are invading already overcrowded parts of the world.[14]

Such disquiet over migration was often behind the demand for measures of population control. Western experts emphasized that population control, not migration, was the answer to the problems faced by the South.

Advocates of immigration control argued that the West bore no responsibility for the population problem of the South. It was suggested that societies which sought to export their population problem were irresponsible. During the forties and fifties, it was commonplace to lecture Asians about the necessity for keeping their house in order and to not expect the West to pay the price for their fecundity. Karl Sax, the influential American Malthusian publicist was blunt and to the point. 'Emigration offers little hope for Asia since the white races occupy or control most of the rest of the world territory', wrote Sax. With a hint of smugness, he added that there was no moral reason why 'nations which control their birth rates in order to maintain a high standard of living should provide for the surplus populations of other countries which breed without consideration of economic and social consequences'.[15]

3.2 The Salience of Race

Studies of differential fertility are fundamentally about perceptions of power, and also touch upon sensitive issues of race and culture. Not surprisingly, they are often guarded in the presentation of their agenda. This point was clearly grasped by the renowned Swedish social scientist Gunnar Myrdal. In a lecture at Harvard University in 1938 he reminded his audience that in the United States, there were 'many elements' which helped to 'complicate, confuse, and emotionally disturb a general discussion of population'. He added, 'one such element is, naturally, the racial and cultural cleavages within this composite nation' (1962, p. 69). Myrdal was aware of the sensitive dimension of this discussion. Views about population in the United States directly touched on racial concerns and therefore tended to be presented in a hesitant and round-about way.

One of the recurrent themes of American demography was the differential rate of growth of its black and white population. Although such monographs were presented in a neutral and technical form, they could not but reveal the underlying concern with the prevailing racial balance. The literature clearly associated power and domestic influence with numerical weight. A variety of factors influencing the rate of population growth were assessed from the standpoint of the outcome of a biological competition. Thus a paper titled 'Fertility of the Negro' observed that diseases which reduce the rate of fertility were 'definitely to the disadvantage of the coloured population' (Kirk, 1942, pp. 60–1). For Dudley Kirk, the author of this study, low levels of fertility implied disadvantage, not because of the health issues but because of the direct link between numbers and power. 'The Negro's importance in American civilisation has been closely related to the size and distribution of the Negro population', he argued (1942, p. 1). What this further implied was that a rise in the 'importance' of one section of the population could only take place at the expense of another.

Those concerned with the maintenance of white superiority, were particularly sensitive to demographic trends. Supporters of Apartheid in South Africa justified racial segregation on the grounds that the realities of differential population growth between black and white required a separate form of development. The argument – that as a result of the 'numerical preponderance of non-whites' and the 'not unfounded fear of being swamped culturally and politically', apartheid made sense – was not contested at an international conference on 'overpopulation' in South Africa in 1970.[16] But even more detached observers believed that differential rates of fertility had important domestic consequences. Contributions in prestigious publications like *Social Forces* and *The American Journal of Sociology* often presented the differential rate of fertility as an expression of an 'interracial struggle'. So a discussion on 'The increasing growth-rate of the Negro population' concluded that as a consequence of this trend 'the Negro problem, instead of decreasing in relative importance, may become serious in the years to come.'[17] There was no need to spell out what this 'problem' was.

The fear that a changing racial balance would create major domestic and international problems motivated some research in the sphere of demography. For example, Frederick Osborn, in his capacity as advisor to the Carnegie Foundation on demographic research, supported an application for the funding of a project on population problems in the British Empire. He reminded the President of the Foundation:'if Mr Carnegie was interested in the British Dominions it was presumably because he believed in the value of the English people who inhabit them, and he therefore would have been concerned at their approaching decline in numbers.'[18] Another Carnegie advisor, Newton D. Baker proposed a major study, which would culminate with the publication of Myrdal's *An American Dilemma: The Negro Problem and Modern Democracy* (1944), because of the 'extraordinary circumstances which led to our having so large a Negro population' (cited in Lagemann, 1992, p. 127). Differential fertility clearly influenced the Carnegie research agenda on both demography and race relations.

After the Second World War, the representation of black population growth as a problem was rarely justified on openly racist grounds. Arguments on this subject tended to become more indirect and circumlocutory. Some writers campaigned for birth control in the black community on the grounds that it would ease racial tensions. From this standpoint, a static number of blacks made for better race relations. The corollary of this view was that the increasing size of the black population would lead to the intensification of racial conflict. The thesis that it was the presence of large numbers of blacks which accounted for race conflict had been fashionable at the turn of the century: 'A primary cause of race friction is the vague, rather intangible, but wholly real feeling of "pressure" which comes to the white man almost instinctively in the presence of a mass of people of a different race. In a certain important sense all racial problems are distinct problems of racial distribution.'[19] Yet, in more subtle forms, this numerical view of race relations continued to influence perceptions in the second half of the century. As late as 1969, for instance, an American mainstream demographer concluded that the rapid growth of the 'non-white' population would 'have tremendous impact and probably operate to exacerbate present racial tension'(Hauser, 1969, p. 100).

If the cause of racial tension was the high growth rate of the black population then the solution which readily suggested itself was birth control. And indeed this was the conclusion drawn by many experts on the subject. As one put it: 'the active encouragement of birth control among the minority group would tend to prevent them having a birth rate higher than that of a majority group, and this in turn would tend to allay anxiety and racial prejudice among the latter' (Flugel, 1947, p. 130). In the post-war era, those who advocated birth control for regulating the size of the black community often justified their position on the ground of commonsense social policy. In the sixties, a leading American demographer, Frank Lorimer contended that the 'greater prolificacy of the non-white population was wholly a function of the relatively less restrained reproductivity of those with meagre schooling'. He added that this 'trend hampers the advance of the nation as a whole, and particularly tends to retard the economic and social advance of non-white communities'.[20] According to Lorimer, the regulation of fertility, through reducing the numbers of the badly educated, would have the effect of ameliorating the position of black people.

Clearly, regardless of individual motives, advocates of population control in the United States were aware that their proposals had important consequences for the domestic racial balance. Gunnar Myrdal's magisterial study of American race relations, *The American Dilemma*, forcefully argued that population policies were inextricably linked to the relation between black and white. His research suggested that both blacks and whites were keen to increase their relative share of the population. Myrdal's writing on this subject is particularly valuable because it openly confronted uncomfortable views, which were rarely expressed in public. Myrdal was insistent that the *'overwhelming majority of white Americans desire that there be as few Negroes as possible in America'*. He added that the flip side of this attitude was that an 'increase of the proportion of Negroes is commonly looked upon as undesirable'. Myrdal also observed that 'almost every Negro' wanted the black population to be 'as large as possible' (1962, pp. 167 and 169). He emphasized that these opinions were 'seldom expressed openly' but, as 'general valuations', they were 'nearly always present'. According to Myrdal, it was this paradox of public silence and private preoccupation that helped explain the strength of the birth control movement in America. Pointing to the American South, where birth control was a taboo subject in public discussion, Myrdal argued that it was the 'presence of the Negroes' which explained the lack of opposition to birth control in practice (1962, see footnote, p. 179). In the South racial concerns overrode moral principles about regulating fertility.

The salience of race for demographic concerns was no less important in the international domain. In international relations before the Second World War, shifts in the balance of population were often interpreted through a racial vocabulary. At the level of global relations, demographic patterns suggested that Western domination faced major long-term obstacles. Many writers on the subject argued that a racial confrontation could only be avoided if the West redistributed some of its resources to benefit the East (see for example Crocker, 1931, and W. S. Thompson, 1929). Myrdal himself warned that time was running out. Pointing to the likely hegemony of the United States in the coming post-Second World War international order, he wrote that 'white peoples will have to adjust to shrinkage while the coloured are bound to expand in

numbers.' For 'perhaps several decades' whites would 'still hold
the lead', and America would be the 'most powerful white nation';
but in the end there would be change (1962, p. 1019). After the War,
Myrdal's call for some sort of adjustment to meet demographic
realities was widely accepted. For some, however, population
control appeared as a viable policy for minimizing the disruptive
effects of international demographic trends. It was in this context,
that the benefits of population policies for the non-industrial world
were first discussed in the industrialized nations.

3.3 North–South Population Tensions: The Cold War and After

It was in the immediate aftermath of the Second World War, that
population growth in the Third World became both a subject of
serious research and a topic of concern for Western policy-makers.
Until this time, public discussion on the subject had been monopolized by alarmist journalism. Although professional demographers often pronounced on the Third World, little research had
been undertaken on population patterns in Africa, Asia or Latin
America. What made mainstream thinkers take this subject seriously
was the recognition that the Western-dominated world system
was unstable. The European empires faced the challenge of anti-
colonial movements. Asia was on the verge of revolt. Moreover, it
was feared that a resurgent Soviet Union could win a significant
constituency of support in Third World societies. It was in this
context that the benefits of population policies for the non-industrial world were first discussed.[21]

Political preoccupations were also marked by economic and
demographic realities. It appeared that the rich nations were
confronted by the rising numbers of the poor. 'Internationally the
fundamental source of conflict, is on the one hand, high birth rates
and poverty and, on the other hand, low birth rates and comparative prosperity', wrote one well-known demographer in 1945.[22]
The fear that have-not countries would demand a better deal from
rich countries with declining populations haunted many of the
influential demographers of the forties. From their perspective,
prevailing demographic patterns contained a conflictual dynamic
which could end in war. Frank Lorimer spoke for many of his
colleagues when he warned that there was 'the alarming prospect

of an intensified international struggle for population as part of a rising obsession with power politics'.[23]

Preventing a North–South population war emerged as an important part of international debate in the forties. There was agreement that a world system organized around empires and colonies only polarized the situation and made a North–South conflict more likely. But what else could be done? Most specialists advocated a policy of making amends for the inequities of the past. Some advocated a redistribution of resources, whilst others suggested support for Third World development.

Lorimer argued that 'the existence of gross inequality in the distribution of population relative to economic resources presents a problem that will plague the conscience of mankind for many generations.' But Lorimer did not appeal merely to the public conscience; he also evoked the spectre of war. 'It may also present the most formidable obstacle to the preservation of peace in the decades that lie ahead', he warned.[24] Other specialists took up the same theme and demanded action before the population problem got out of hand. Warren Thompson wrote ominously about the international consequences of differential fertility, observing that 'we may have been justified in ignoring such a differential growth in population in the past when it was working to the advantage of the Western European peoples, but we can scarcely afford to do so in the future.' Thompson demanded that the West accommodate the anti-colonial aspirations of the people of Asia:

> if we still hold most of this region as colonies and continue to exploit them as we are now doing, will they continue to be as subservient as in the past? Is it not time that we began to take account of this new differential in population growth and for the sake of expediency, if we are not moved by considerations of justice.[25]

This was also the argument adopted by Dudley Kirk. 'To the extent that numbers are a factor in the distribution of economic and political power', he contended, 'there will be some redistribution of power from old to new centres.'[26] The draining of power away from the West was anticipated by virtually everyone involved in the field of demography.

Western fears about the consequences of differential fertility between the North and the South acquired a novel form during the Cold War. Those concerned about strategic demography became obsessed with the possibility that the Soviet Union might use population to its advantage. Would the multitude of the dispossessed find a new champion in the Soviet Union? This was the question posed time and again. In a nightmare scenario billions of resentful people from the South combined with Soviet organization and technology against a feeble and declining West. It was felt that, in the population war, the Soviet Union possessed the advantage of not being tainted with an imperialist past. Moreover, the Soviet Union was said to have its cultural roots in the East, and could therefore expect to benefit from the emergence of anti-Western sentiment.[27]

In retrospect, it is surprising just how unconfident Western policy-makers felt about the outcome of competition with the Soviet Union for the loyalty of the Third World. Many specialists believed that desperate societies facing formidable economic obstacles would gravitate towards the Soviet Bloc. Kingsley Davis, a central figure in the American debate about population, argued that the West was 'handicapped in its appeal to backward areas'. According to Davis, the conditions that prevailed in Third World societies – mass poverty, resentment against domination – assisted Soviet diplomatic efforts to succeed in the Cold War. Under these circumstances 'the demographic problems of the underdeveloped countries' made 'these nations more vulnerable to Communism'. According to this perspective, large numbers of dissatisfied African and Asian youth served to intensify conflict and instability. They would constitute a ready-made audience for radical movements, intent on challenging the world order.[28]

Linking the Cold War to Third World population growth was an influential theme in the non-specialist literature. John Robbins's *Too Many Asians* (1959) was representative of the journalistic publications of the period. According to Robbins, the 'root' of Asia's 'problem of population' was 'copulation'. Worse, the densely populated societies of Asia might turn against the West. To illustrate his warning, Robbins used the Indian state of Kerala as a case study. In 1957, the people of Kerala elected a Communist government. Many Western observers saw this event as the confirmation of their worst fears. According to Robbins, the crucial variable was 'overpopulation'. With more than a hint of hyperbole, he observed: 'Kerala is so overcrowded that its people simply do not have enough food to keep them living above concentration-camp level.' People living in such a 'great tropical poorhouse' had in desperation, turned to 'anyone who would promise them relief from their hunger and poverty'. Therefore, Robbins believed, there was a direct correlation between the rates of population growth and the influence of subversive forces. He predicted that the countries 'most plagued by overpopulation and facing the dimmest prospects of relief' would be 'the ones most likely to fall' to the forces of Communism (1959, pp. 12, 13 and 17).

The integration of strategic demography into Cold War ideology, was not restricted to sensationalist authors like Robbins, who wrote for a mass audience. Leading academics and experts shared the view that population trends in the Third World could prove decisive to the waging of the Cold War. This point was reiterated at academic conferences as well as behind the closed doors of influential think tanks. Philip Hauser, the director of the Population Research Centre at the University of Chicago, former president of the Population Association of America, of the American Sociological Association and of the American Statistical Association as well as an influential government advisor, personified the approach of the American population establishment to the Cold War. In the sixties, Hauser actively endorsed the linkage of population to the Cold War. He argued that 'the outcome of the Cold War, in large measure, may depend on the ability of the developing nations to control their rates of population growth.' According to Hauser, population growth was a major obstacle to the economic development of the Third World. And without economic development, impoverished societies would experience instability and social unrest. Hauser believed that such societies would find the 'blandishments of the communist world' irresistible (1969, p. 27).

The grafting of Cold War themes on to traditional population concerns reflected the temper of the times. It was difficult to avoid getting caught up in the Cold War; indeed, one sure way of gaining publicity for a cause was to emphasize its relevance for the Cold War. This insight was not lost on those who were concerned with the outcome of differential rates of fertility on a world scale. No doubt many advocates of population control argued for their position through an opportunistic use of the Cold War vocabulary. This casual and manipulative use of Cold War concerns can be found in many contributions on the subject. For example, Paul Ehrlich's best-seller, *The Population Bomb*, could not resist the temptation to supplement its main argument with Cold War themes. Ehrlich offered a vision of the future in which chronic instability in the Third World inexorably led to the triumph of Communist regimes. His writings are peppered with futuristic visions of such outcomes. In one imaginary scenario projected for 1979, 'the last non-Communist government in Latin America, that of Mexico, is replaced by a Chinese supported military junta' (1971, pp. 39–40).

For most writers on the subject, the real issue at stake was the threat posed by the growth of the population of the South. In a sense it is possible to argue that the Cold War allowed this threat to be made more intelligible to a larger audience then before. It is interesting to note that even the most intense representations of Cold War population problems remained subject to the more fundamental assumptions about North–South demographic conflicts. Often, Western writers made a distinction between the Western and the Asian population problem. The main focus of concern was 'overpopulated' China. Indeed it was often suggested, that ideological considerations were less significant than demographic realities and that it was only a matter of time before the Soviet Union would also become scared by the population of China. Kingsley Davis wrote in 1959, that Moscow was frightened by the threat of Chinese ascendancy. The dimension of this spectre was spelled out by Davis in the following terms: 'China, with a projected 1975 population almost double the expected figures for the United States and Russia combined, would be the strongest contender for world leadership. Such a mass, equipped with modern arms and disciplined by a dictatorship, if bent on conquest, could be stopped only by a united world outside.'[29] For Davis, ideological considerations clearly gave way to unity with the Soviet Union against China. Issues of race and culture continued to lurk behind the agenda of the Cold War.

Davis's views on the implications of Sino–Soviet conflict were an accepted part of Western demographic consciousness. Philip Hauser speculated that the fundamental source of global conflict was North–South rather than the ideological East–West rivalry between the superpowers. He believed that the tension between China and the Soviet Union could intensify the conflict between the have and the have-not nations of the world. 'It is not impossible that the USSR will find she has more in common with the have than with the have-not nations', argued Hauser (1969, p. 28). That many Western anti-Communist experts felt a degree of affinity with the Soviet Union in its rivalry with China, illustrates the continuity of their population fears.

The centrality of perceptions of North–South conflict in the population agenda continued into the nineties. Since the eighties, Northern fears about Southern population trends have become a more pervasive feature of international affairs. Western, particularly American strategists have replaced the population-Cold War linkage with a more elementary geopolitical perspective. It is argued that demographic trends place in jeopardy Western access to important natural resources. Alternatively it is suggested that issues of security are at stake, since Western power will inevitably diminish in response to demographic realities. This was the fear expressed among others by the American National Security Council's Ad Hoc Group on Population Policy in 1980. Over the following fifteen years, numerous committees of experts drew similar conclusions.[30]

With the decline of the Cold War, problems associated with the South have been elevated to the top of the international relations agenda. Increasingly, the Third World is held responsible for most manifestations of global instability. A variety of issues – fundamentalism, environmental degradation, terrorism, political instability – are now routinely linked with population growth. The danger of the nuclear bomb of the Cold War has been replaced by the 'demographic bomb' of Third World societies.

The continued decline of fertility in the West has led to a renewed emphasis on the topic of population relativities. Paul Demeny, former vice-president of the Population Council, sees the danger of Third World population growth in classical social-Darwinian terms. According to Demeny, differential rates of fertility are a major source of concern from the point of view of the slower growing nations. Why? Because 'In the domain of evolutionary theory, the consequence of any sustained difference between the rates of growth of two populations occupying the same ecological niche is straightforward: the eventual complete displacement of the slower growing by the faster growing one' (cited in P. J. Donaldson, 1990 p. 24). From this standpoint, the trends of population growth suggest that global relations are moving towards conflict. This conflict assumes an ominous significance when the two contrasting trajectories of population growth are brought into a relation with each other.

The increasingly globalist imagination of the late twentieth century has strengthened insecurities about population relativities. Consequently, the population bomb ticking away in the South is translated into an 'immigration crisis' in Europe and the United States. Paul Kennedy expressed this drama in the following terms: 'As the better-off families of the northern hemisphere individually decided that having only one or at the most two children is sufficient, they may not recognise that they are in a small way vacating future space (that is, jobs, parts of inner cities, shares of population, shares of market preferences) to faster-growing ethnic groups both inside and outside their national boundaries' (Kennedy, 1993, p. 45). Others too have argued this thesis as a prelude to demanding new forms of regulation for controlling the movement of people. The explosion of concern with immigration in the West in the nineties is clearly not unconnected with the focus on the population problem of the South.

3.4 The Argument

Population panics have been an integral part of Western consciousness for some time. In different periods, such responses have been influenced by a variety of experiences. Unfortunately, studies of population debates have often ignored the wider influences on the discussion. Even critics of Western demographic consciousness find it difficult to step outside the terms in which discussions on populations are framed. So for example, some critics of Western population policy share a common premise regarding the importance of numbers. Their position is often the mirror-image of the Western population control lobby. In some cases they even support population growth because they feel that it will challenge Western domination. So Bondestam argued that 'the more potentially exploited and unemployed people that are born, the stronger the subversive forces of society will grow.'[31] From this standpoint the pressure of large numbers becomes the vehicle for change.

Other critics of population control interpret this policy in its own terms and fail to consider how it fits into a wider agenda. For example, an interesting pro-natalist text by the right-wing American economist Jacqueline Kasun cannot comprehend the impulse behind Washington's policies. She argues that American foreign interests are fundamentally inconsistent with its population policy towards the South. 'Those who imagine that foreign population control serves the cause of American "imperialism" are quite mistaken. On the contrary, the programs . . . impose significant costs on the United States . . . not only of money but of goodwill in sensitive areas' (1988, p. 94). However Kasun finds it difficult to account for the sheer consistency with which this 'mistaken' policy has been pursued. Despite her considerable insights, she remains oblivious to the relation between Washington's perception of the balance of global power and its support for population control.

The aim of this chapter was to examine some of the wider influences of the role of demographic consciousness in North–South relations. An examination of Western contributions on the subject indicates that their focus has been on the balance of power between the North and the South. Anxieties about population were responses to the sense of losing power. The issue was not simply whether power had actually been lost – the fear of decline was sufficient for the construction of the most elaborate demographic nightmares. Historians have pointed out that, often, it was a sense of social impasse which generated a panic about population. For the historian E. H. Carr, the imposition of immigration control in the United States in the twenties symbolized the exhaustion of society. He argued that it was the 'symbol of a world grown static and stereotyped' (1944, p. 106).

In the end, the fear of population growth is inseparable from the conviction that any shift in the balance of power between the North and the South will be at the expense of the former. The sense that the West has much to lose permeates its demographic consciousness. The French demographer, Alfred Sauvy (1969, p. 334) helped to clarify this sentiment, when he observed:

> Opinion in the West is now conscious of the fast demographic growth in the Third World. Large scale publicity is given to the 'rise of the coloured people' or to the swarming of the hungry; Westerners feel rather like masters or servants in a castle, watching great masses of ragged people multiplying in the countryside around, obviously to no good intent.[32]

The wider preoccupations with loss of authority, the fear of retribution, maybe even a sense of shame about the past, interweave with more specific population issues and help shape the North's obsession with the numbers of the South.

Between the North and the South, the issue of demography has rarely been a neutral technical matter. How and why a population agenda comes to be set is itself a subject worthy of investigation. Possibly such an investigation will help modify some of the prevailing views on the subject.

4

Forging the Connection between Population and Development

In contemporary discussions, it is generally assumed that there exists an important connection between population and development and commentators often act as if this relationship were self-evident. This chapter suggests that the terms of the relationship, if indeed there is a relationship, are far from clear.

The conceptualization of a relationship between population and development is a relatively recent one. Until the final phase of the Second World War there was relatively little discussion of any link between the two variables. The attempt to establish a connection between population growth and underdevelopment is the subject of this chapter.

The elaboration of a distinct academic discipline of development studies was strongly influenced by concern with the population growth of the South. Indeed, before the Second World War, the literature on population problems in the South was far more prominent than studies of economic development. In the United States, many of the leading demographers became interested in the issue of economic development because they believed that socio-economic advance was the condition for stabilizing the rate of fertility in the colonial world. According to the dominant paradigm of the time, that of demographic transition, 'fertility would only fall as a result of the cumulative mutually reinforcing spectrum of effects consequent on full-scale industrialisation and modernisation.'[1] From this perspective, development was seen as a precondition for overcoming the population problem. As the discussion will show, development was supported not so much for its own sake, but because it was believed that industrialization would lead to a decline in the rate of fertility. Those who were absorbed by the issue of population growth regarded development mainly as a means to an end. Their attitude towards development was instrumentalist and highly pragmatic. As will be seen, the goal of population stabilization invariably took precedence over that of development.

This chapter explores the elaboration of the connection between development and population growth. This intellectual project was always fraught with tension and soon became the subject of controversy, as demographers disagreed about what exactly the relationship was. The definition of the problem underwent substantial modification. It is possible to identify at least two distinct characterizations of the relationship between development and population growth.

PARADIGM 1. In the forties, demographers identified population growth as the problem facing the societies of the South. They argued that a solution, indeed the only solution to this problem, was that of economic development.

PARADIGM 2. During the fifties a more pessimistic paradigm emerged. It was suggested that population was growing too fast for development to occur. The new consensus was that population growth had to be checked so that the economy could develop. In this paradigm the problem was that of development and the solution was that of population control.

The shift in paradigm was never complete and the discussion often lacked clarity. However, an examination of this shift may provide important insights into the evolution of demographic and development themes.

4.1 Demography's Influence on the Meaning of Development

One of the key propositions being argued for here is that Western concern with population growth in the South has strongly influenced the very meaning of development. From the outset, concern with population shaped the evolution of the debate on the conceptualization of development and the academic disciplines that emerged around this subject.

It was during the forties that post-war planners, academics and politicians began seriously to address the problem of development in the societies of the South. Population was not the only influence on the emerging development literature. Many writers have pointed to the important role played by Western anxieties about the destabilizing consequences of endemic poverty in Africa and Asia. Others have emphasized the centrality of the American Cold War policy of containment in the elaboration of development policies. Critics of liberal development theory have suggested that American leaders were motivated by the fear that anti-colonial reactions to economic exploitation and foreign domination would benefit the Soviet Union. Such leaders therefore encouraged the economic development of the Third World in order to diffuse anti-colonial protest. Writing in this vein, Hunt has argued that 'development was the younger sibling of containment.'[2]

Among the many factors that have shaped the construction of the development agenda, the importance of population fears has often been underestimated. Indeed, some have gone so far as to argue that demography was tangential to the evolution of the development agenda. According to Barbara Duden, while population eventually became central to the field of development, 'in the 1950s demographers were still on the fringes of the developmental discourse.'[3] This periodization of the discussion is open to question. The post-war development agenda was from the outset directly influenced by anxieties about rapid population growth in the South. That is why there were so many demographers among those who first self-consciously formulated development as a desirable policy for Third World societies. In any case, the issues which were isolated as critical – poverty, instability, anti-colonial revolts – were often perceived through the medium of the pressure of population.[4] Terms like 'population bomb' and 'teeming masses' expressed the sentiment that this was a threat that the West ignored at its peril.

During the earlier, interwar era, the unequal division of the globe, differential rates of fertility and access to resources were often treated as interrelated problems. In 1929, Warren Thompson, one of the pioneers of demographic transition theory, adopted this approach in his influential text, *Danger Spots in World Population*. Thompson was worried about the consequences of a situation where the world was dominated by a handful of Western powers, who were insensitive to the needs of the colonial world. Thompson believed that such a state of affairs could easily culminate in conflict and war. For Thompson, population pressure was a danger that directly contributed to global conflict. He noted:

> What is meant here by 'danger spots in population' is then, areas on the earth of greatly different population pressure as measured by the relation of people to resources. The attempt by people either living in low-pressure areas or holding such areas as dependencies for their own exclusive use, to keep the people living in high-pressure areas pent up within their present boundaries indefinitely is what is likely to cause trouble (1929, p. 13).

Thompson argued that the only way to avoid the destabilizing consequences of population growth was through a global redistribution of resources in favour of the poor regions of the world.

DEMOGRAPHIC TRANSITION

The theory of demographic transition, first outlined by Warren Thompson and later elaborated by other demographers, sought to explain why all industrialised countries passed through a similar pattern of population growth.

Until modernization, all societies experienced a similar pattern of population growth. This was the outcome of circumstances which prevailed in pre-industrial societies, where both the rates of fertility and of mortality were high. In this Stage 1, the high rates of death cancelled out the effects of the high rates of birth. According to the theory, the onset of modernization created a new relationship between fertility and mortality. Improvements in sanitation, diet and public health contributed to the reduction in mortality. In this new demographic regime, Stage 2, life expectancy was substantially increased. However, at the early phase of modernization, the fall in the death rate was not matched by a decline in the rate of fertility. So the high rates of birth of the pre-industrial era persisted, but not the high rate of death. The consequence of this divergence between the rates of fertility and of mortality was a major growth of population. Consequently, the immediate effect of modernization in Europe was to undermine the previous regime of demographic stability and initiate a period of rapid population growth. According to the theory of demographic transition, Stage 2 came to an end when the process of modernization began to influence the rate of fertility.

In Stage 3, the combined impact of modernization, urbanization and industrialism led to a decline in birth rates. Thus by the end of the nineteenth century, the reduction in the rates of birth was evident in Europe; falling levels of fertility now converged with lower death rates.

Redistribution of resources combined with policies designed to stimulate economic growth was perceived as the means for easing the pressure of population growth. This, in turn, was expected to weaken the dynamic towards global conflict.

It was clear to most specialists that transition theory had to be adapted and reworked in relation to the circumstances which prevailed in underdeveloped societies. For example, unlike in the West, high rates of population growth prevailed in underdeveloped societies, even before industrialization. Demographers thus worked out a new colonial version of transition theory. According to this 'colonial explanation', the population pressure experienced by the regions of the South, was the consequence of the distorted character of the modernization process. Unlike in the West, the reduction in the rate of mortality preceded industrialization. It was suggested that in the colonies, government policy and not economic change, brought down the levels of mortality. However, because the imperial powers regarded their colonies as merely markets for their goods, they discouraged industrialization. But there could be no modernization without industrialization. The conditions necessary for a decline of fertility – urbanization, creation of a wage labour force, family nucleation – did not exist. Hence, change in the colonial context brought down the rate of mortality without effecting fertility. In particular, change did not create the socio-cultural framework which in the West was consistent with reducing fertility. The result of this process, it was argued, was a population explosion. Thompson observed, that population growth was 'the Malthusian dilemma of all colonialism'. The solution proposed by Thompson was development. He argued that 'the colonies should be aided in the development of a better balanced economy' (1946, p. 312). It was this expectation of rapid population growth in the colonial world that underlined the urgency of promoting positive policies of economic development.

According to most accounts, the first monographs on the theory of economic development of non-industrialized societies were published in 1944, and it was only after the war that publications on economic development became fairly common.[5] As late as 1949, a leading economist employed by the Secretariat of the United Nations could write that one 'cannot fail to be struck by the extraordinary neglect' of underdeveloped countries by his colleagues.[6] By contrast, demographers were more directly concerned with the societies of the colonial world. It is worth noting that some of the earliest contributions on the subject of the development of

Africa, Asia and Latin America were made by demographers. By the mid-forties, there existed a theoretical synthesis which linked the prevailing pattern of population growth to the process of modernization. This was the adaptation of the theory of demographic transition to the task of explaining the peculiar relationship between population growth and modernization in the colonies.

4.2 Rapid Development as a Solution to High Fertility

From the outset, the concept of development presupposed the attainment of Western attitudes towards fertility. The concept of development that was in general use in the West was not reducible to economic growth alone. During the forties and fifties, this concept was often interchangeable with the term Westernization. The term development, like Westernization implicitly touched upon the domain of attitudes and values. For demographers and other specialists, one of the main virtues of development was that it would challenge the value system that supported a traditional orientation towards high rates of fertility. Modernization theorists believed that economic change would deal a fatal blow to the extended family system and encourage a trend towards the spread of small couple-based nuclear families. Consequently, many experts regarded development as an effective, if indirect, form of fertility control.

It was generally accepted that agricultural societies with high rates of mortality tended to support a regime of high rates of fertility. Prerequisites for the emergence of an aspiration for small families are industrialization and urbanization. Such changes help to create a situation where parents no longer require large numbers of children to provide support and security. In the forties and fifties, writers on the subject hoped that development would help transform the prevailing traditional attitudes towards fertility in the South. Kingsley Davis, one of the most influential American demographers of the post-war era, anticipated that it would undermine the traditional attitudes towards fertility in Asia. He predicted in 1945, that Asians 'will acquire modern civilisation in time to check their fertility and thus achieve an efficient demographic balance'.[7]

Modern civilization and development implied the establishment of the kind of social structures which, in Europe, went hand in hand with a decline in the rate of fertility. 'There is a clear consensus among students of population problems that industrialisation, urbanisation and education are the three prerequisites for a reduction in fertility', wrote Frank Lorimer. Lorimer added that it was only when there was a widespread belief in the possibility of economic advance, that the motivation for birth control would exist.[8] The central role assigned to the promotion of education and urbanization along with industrialization was a testimony to the importance Lorimer and his colleagues attached to shifting attitudes and cultural practices.

For some writers, the impact of development on levels of fertility was actually more important than its effect on overcoming poverty and economic stagnation. According to one well-known commentator on the subject, there were two reasons why industrialization was a desirable policy for every part of the underdeveloped world:

> first, it will increase the productivity of labour and create an abundance of badly needed commodities and services and transform over a period of time the present economy of scarcity and under-utilisation of resources into an economy of possible full employment and self-sufficiency, if not abundance; secondly, and this is probably more important for these countries, industrialisation will encourage, if properly planned, the development of new urban patterns of living which lead to the control of the high birth rate.[9]

The emphasis placed on the impact that economic development would have on fertility was based on the conviction that high rates of population growth were the principal danger.

The belief that the rate of population growth was threatening disaster influenced the way that economic development was conceptualized. Frank Notestein, the Director of the Population Division of the United Nations, questioned whether 'economic development can come rapidly enough to forestall catastrophes'. The catastrophes he had in mind were clearly related to the high rates of fertility of Asia.[10] The view that economic development was involved in a race against time before the population bomb exploded was prominent in the literature. In the case of Notestein, words like 'urgency' and the need to forestall a 'tragedy' are linked not just to development but to 'rapid economic development'.

It is interesting to note that the term 'rapid economic development' reoccurred regularly in the reviews of the so-called population problem. As Davis argued, 'the faster the role of modernisation, other things being equal, the quicker will be the response of fertility, the earlier the end to population growth, the smaller the ultimate population reached, and the higher the eventual level of living.'[11] The focus on rapidity indicated the consciousness of running out of time. It also suggested that before anything else, economic development had to address the issue of population pressure. The logic of this linkage of development and population was to regard economic growth as a form of indirect mechanism of fertility control. This was the accepted orientation of most works on population problems. Kingsley Davis's, 1951 study, *The population of India and Pakistan*, exemplified this approach. 'Now we are considering rapid industrialisation as a population policy', wrote Davis. He added, that as such, 'it is really a means of reducing fertility, not directly through officially diffusing contraceptive material and information, but indirectly through changing the conditions of life and thus forcing people in their private capacity to seek the means of family limitations' (1951, p. 229). Thus for Davis, economic development was a means for achieving the goal of population control.

The significance which demographers attached to the rapidity of economic development was based on the belief that it was dangerous to wait for fertility to adjust to the falling levels of mortality. It was feared that by the time levels of fertility began to decline in response to the stimulus of modernization, the levels of population of many colonial societies would prove to be far too high. Some demographers expressed deep anxieties about the possibility that the population growth experienced in the wake of Western industrialization in Stage 2 of its demographic transition would be also repeated in modernizing colonial societies. Only this time, because population growth rates were already high, the outcome of Stage 2 would be devastating. In this sense, Hauser expressed the hope that the Third World would not follow the demographic patterns that characterized Western industrialization. For Hauser, the fundamental problem was whether it was 'possible for a pre-industrial or primitive culture to receive the benefits of "modern civilisation" without producing the cycle of population change experienced by the Western world'. This outlook implied speeding up fertility control 'so as to cut down the gap experienced in the Western world between decreasing mortality and the decline in the birth rate'.[12] In practice, this meant doing everything necessary to accelerate family nucleation.

The presentiment that time was running out, particularly in

Asia, inspired many specialists to demand resources for broad cultural change. 'In Asia numbers are so great, the pressure of people on subsistence so intense, that time is crucial', wrote Irene Taeuber. She warned that Asia could not 'afford to permit the transition from high to low fertility to evolve as a by-product of the pressures and the stimuli generated by the urbanisation process'. According to Taeuber, everything depended on the 'rapidity of the cultural developments' through which Asians would adjust their reproduction to economic realities.[13]

It is worth noting that advocates of rapid economic development never reflected on the practicalities of their proposals. At a time when economic growth in the colonial world was anything but rapid, the failure to consider the mechanics and the strategy of development seems both careless and naive. What is the explanation for this disengagement from the nuts and bolts of economic development? The most plausible answer is that demographers had an essentially instrumental interest in economic development. Their energies were absorbed by the problem of population growth. Their elevation of rapid development was not the product of deliberation about a viable economic strategy, it was the outcome of the demographic consciousness which feared that time was running out. At times, the instrumental approach towards development verged on the manipulative. For example, Davis supported 'rapid industrialisation' in Asia, because it was far more likely to be accepted by the relevant governments than the policy of birth control. The policy of industrialization was consistent with the aspirations of Asian elites. That their aspiration was motivated by the demands of economic growth rather than the impulse of population control did not matter to Davis. 'The one measure that has the best chance of being pushed is rapid industrialisation, but not for demographic reasons', concluded Davis (1951, p. 231). Davis, along with his colleagues, was prepared to run with the rapid industrialization strategy in order to advance the cause close to their heart, that of population control.

4.3 Population Growth as an Obstacle to Development

The way in which American demographers conceptualized development was a contradictory one. If, indeed, there was a race between the rates of population and economic growth, then how could societies afford the luxury of waiting for the benefits of development? From this perspective, development was a long-term ideal with minimal consequences for solving the population problem in the here and now. Bit by bit, as the climate of discussion changed, this sentiment became dominant among demographers. There can be little doubt that by the late forties, this was the consensus amongst the leading American and British specialists on the subject. According to one recent study of the emergence of this new consensus, it was the victory of the Chinese revolution in 1949 which led to this reassessment of the viability of development as a solution to population problems.[14]

At the time, the American Milbank Memorial Fund regularly brought together the leading demographers to consider the relationship between population and development in non-industrialized societies. According to Symonds and Carder, this group 'became the main protagonist of the view that economic development alone would not bring about a spontaneous fall in the birth rate of less developed countries and that ways would therefore have to be found of inducing social changes which would encourage smaller families' (1973, p. 52). The composition of this group – which included Frank Notestein, the director of the Population Division of the United Nations – ensured that this consensus had a major influence on the discussion internationally.

The view that the population problem could not rely entirely on economic growth implicitly questioned the relevance of development for the control of fertility. This question mark over whether development could save the day was always a sub-plot evident in the literature. In the forties, it ran alongside the elaboration of the concept of development. The way in which demographic transition was theorized in relation to the colonial context raised important questions about the relationship between economic and population growth. The view that development was a solution to the problem existed in an uneasy relation with the sentiment that prevailing demographic patterns doomed economic progress from the start. Some of the optimistic views about the capacity of economic development to check population growth were qualified by the assumption that in colonial societies the situation was too out of control. The more pessimistic demographers contended that change in Asia and Africa influenced levels of mortality but not of fertility. Moreover, they argued that the already high levels of population acted as a barrier to economic growth. Thus, it was suggested, that particularly in Asia, the benefits of economic change would be dissipated by the explosion in the numbers of people.

In the post-war era, the view that high levels of population were an obstacle to development came to be supported by some influential economists associated with the United Nations. Hans Singer reinterpreted the traditional concept of the Malthusian trap to argue that there were serious obstacles facing development. He believed that the immediate outcome of improvement in the quality of life was the lowering of the death rate. The increase of population that would follow this process, he argued, would 'use up the increment in production, leaving no room for investment'. This pessimistic account of the consequence of change, led to the conclusion that colonial societies were in danger of not being able to make the transition to a regime of low birth rates. Singer noted:

> It is highly probable, in view of the experience of industrialised countries that sustained development and industrialisation might result in a lowering of birth rates, thus releasing sources of investment. That blissful stage, however, is never reached because the immediate effect of small improvements is such as to throw the underdeveloped country back to its starting point. Development under such conditions is like trying to run up a downward-moving escalator. If you could only move from your original position, you could get off the escalator and go forward without difficulty; but once on the escalator you are prevented from obtaining freedom of motion.[15]

Such a pessimistic prognosis of the prospects for development was by no means typical of the economic literature of the late forties. The presentiment that development contained a fatal flaw was much more characteristic of those more specifically involved with demography.

A new nightmare scenario emerged alongside the elaboration of a development agenda. This scenario projected a situation where the fall in the death rates brought by change would lead to a further growth of population. This would cancel out the benefits of growth. Irene Taeuber feared that 'if the East follows the West, the initial effect of the industrial and agricultural developments essential to the increase of product will be further decreases in mortality and an accelerated rate of natural increase.' For Taeuber, this increase in the rate of fertility constituted a real menace. She was convinced that it would prevent a rise in the standard of living, which in turn would slow down 'the diffusion of patterns and values' that lead to the slowing of fertility.[16] The conclusion which stemmed from this analysis was that high levels of population counteracted the potentially beneficial effects of economic growth. The view that population growth held back the process of development and the modernization of lifestyles was gradually taking shape.

This nightmare scenario acquired a sharp focus in the work of Notestein. Notestein was alarmed by the possibility that economic growth would be too superficial to effect fertility. He wrote of the 'danger' of a situation where there was 'only moderate economic and sanitary improvement unaccompanied by the social changes that affect fertility'. In such circumstances economic change would merely stimulate population growth and do nothing for undermining the attitudes that supported high rates of fertility. Changes that could make a real difference were 'difficult to achieve unless economic development' was 'rapid enough to lift the level of living in spite of substantial population increase'. Notestein added: 'If gains in production only match those in population growth, "improvement" may result principally in ever larger masses of humanity living close to the margins of existence and vulnerable to every shock in the world economic and political structure. Such "progress" may amount to setting the stage for calamity'.[17] This alarmist account of the consequences of change had important implications for those concerned with the problem of population. Notestein had implicitly renounced development as an effective option for reducing the rates of fertility. If anything, the combination of high rates of population growth with a pre-industrial setting had placed a question mark over the viability of the process of modernization itself. In these circumstances, modernization, and in particular the spread of the nuclear family, would remain an elusive goal.

In a stimulating retrospective contribution on this discussion, Dennis Hodgson has pointed to the shift away from a developmentalist perspective in Notestein's thinking. Hodgson remarked that Notestein 'came to consider population growth itself a stumbling block to economic development'. Consequently 'active intervention to lower fertility was needed if there was to be economic development.'[18] Others too followed Notestein's trajectory. For many demographers, it seemed simply too impractical to rely on the long-term changes brought about by economic development. They came to believe that societies which possessed a high level of population could not provide the foundation for dynamic development.

The disenchantment with the indirect method of curbing growth through development created an interest in other options of fertility control. There was a growing interest in influencing the system of beliefs that supported large families. The developmentalist paradigm of the mid-forties suggested that attitudes towards fertility altered as a consequence of socio-economic change. This was contested by the new pessimistic prognosis regarding the outcome of socio-economic change. More generally, many experts reacted against the indirect method of structural change through development. There was a discernible move towards policies that promised to influence fertility directly. Such policies aspired towards a process of modernization but without development.

4.4 Isolating Traditional Culture

With this change of orientation, cultural attitudes towards reproduction were increasingly treated as a variable that existed independently of socio-economic forces. This shift in paradigm expressed the lack of faith in development. It also represented a tentative exercise in damage limitation. But, because of its reactive character and lack of analytical reflection it also lacked intellectual coherence. Kingsley Davis sounded less than convinced when he observed that although in the 'past the reduction of fertility had to wait upon the growth of industry' the pattern of fertility 'should not be regarded as inherently unmodifiable in the early stages of industrialisation'. Davis speculated that it might be possible to modify attitudes of 'traditional cultures' towards fertility, though he conceded that 'evidence is admittedly scarce.'[19] It certainly was not new evidence or new analysis but a loss of faith in the process of modernization that motivated the shift in paradigm. New means had to be found to control population growth. The new interest in modifying traditional views of fertility showed that the commitment to development was at best pragmatic.

The reorientation of research towards the investigation of traditional values and beliefs was motivated by the question of why people failed to adjust their fertility so that it would converge with the falling death rate. There was more than a suspicion that the real culprit was the traditional culture of Africa and Asia, which appeared to celebrate large families. Western experts argued that non-industrial attitudes towards fertility were deeply embedded in the societies of the South. Hertzler blamed the extended family structure for supporting an inappropriate reproductive behaviour. He contended, that the extended family was a problem because it celebrated the offspring as 'agents of ancestor worship' and thereby it gave a 'tremendous religious stimulus to high fertility' (1956, p. 140).

The concentration on cultural values led to tautological conclusions. Contributions on the topic tended to say little beyond stating that people had positive attitudes towards high levels of fertility because of their system of beliefs. The more socio-economic factors were left out of the picture, the more cultural values acquired an autonomy and a momentum of their own. Increasingly, rates of fertility were no longer perceived as a constituent part of people's accommodation to their environment and circumstance, but as an arbitrary artifice of culture. The cultural mode of explanation portrayed population levels as the product of the peculiar customs of the people concerned. In this model, the rational Western attitude towards fertility was counterposed to the irrational practices of other societies.

'Rational control of fertility within marriage is barely on the horizon in any African society', wrote Lorimer in the early fifties. Lorimer suggested that despite social change, some African people preserved their 'primitive social organization'. These traditional organizations, which emphasized fertility, have remained in force, thus continuing to boost the levels of population.[20] This construction of a distinct type of African fertility helped to recast the problem away from the issue of development towards the reproductive habits of traditional peoples. Tackling the problem of the 'culture of high fertility' was placed at the top of the demographic agenda. Modernization, which primarily meant the adoption of Western values, especially in the realm of family life, emerged as the principal issue in development studies.

The separation of the pattern of fertility growth from socio-economic trends had a number of important consequences. It first of all meant that the culture of fertility could be treated in its own right. Through the elevation of Western patterns of reproduction to an absolute standard, fertility was characterized as rational or irrational regardless of the specific circumstances in which people lived. If fertility was constituted in its own terms, then population policies could be deployed to educate people to adopt more rational attitudes towards reproduction. This was the approach increasingly supported by the population establishment in the fifties and sixties. The other important consequence of the privileged position assigned to a culture of fertility was that it reversed the conceptual relationship between development and population. Development lost its appeal as a solution to the problem of population. On the contrary the elimination of traditional attitudes towards fertility was now proposed as the precondition for successful development. Increasingly population policies were advocated on the ground that they were the key to overcoming the obstacles to the development of the societies of Africa, Asia and Latin America. Logically, this implied that modernization – especially a change in the system of values – had to precede development.

4.5 An Intellectual Impasse

Despite the many shifts in the emphasis of demographic debate throughout this century, the overall tendency in the post-war era was to link the population problem to that of development. Population was now less and less represented as a racial or geopolitical issue. It was widely discussed within the context of post-war reconstruction, as one of a number of technical problems. Population pressure was now represented as an economic problem, which, in the non-industrial world, doomed people to poverty. The corollary of this view was that population control resulted in significant economic benefits. Demographers now argued for specific population policies with reference to their contribution for economic development.

The arguments of demographers, as discussed so far in this chapter, had as their premise the vision of a population explosion in the South. This was an alarmist scenario, which projected a Malthusian nightmare into the not too distant future. But what was the basis for these arguments? Although demographers confidently held forth on the population problem of this or that region, their arguments lacked substantiation from the realm of facts. Most speculation about demographic trends was based on the recognition that the continuing decline in mortality would create an ever widening gap between the birth and the death rates. Demographers argued that unless birth rates also fell, a population explosion would ensue.

Hard information on the demographic patterns of the non-industrialized world was conspicuous by its absence. Richard

Gardner, who was an American delegate to the UN, recalled that when its Population Commission 'met for the first time in 1947, demographic statistics were so incomplete that it was hardly possible to speak of world population problems' (cited in S. P. Johnson, 1987, p. xxii). Yet, the absence of reliable information did not in any way inhibit the experts of the day from regularly pronouncing on world population problems. Five years later, in 1953, a UN report, *The determinants and consequences of population trends*, conceded that the situation as regards demographic data had not improved. It reported that 'statistical data on fertility are lacking for many parts of the world and particularly is this true of most underdeveloped countries where such data are urgently needed for the planning of economic and social development' (United Nations, 1953, p. 96).

Facts did not need to intrude on the debate on the population problem. As the UN report delicately reminded its audience, 'discussion of controversial questions could be made more fruitful were better statistics assembled' (p. 284). The British based demographer, Kuczynski was more blunt about the consequences of the absence of reliable information on the demography in Africa. To form a correct opinion on demographic matters without conclusive figures is well-nigh impossible because demographic facts are not obvious. To appraise fertility, mortality or migrations is about as difficult in most African dependencies as to appraise the frequency of adultery in this country' (1948, p. vi). Demographers, nevertheless continued to speculate about the peculiar character of African fertility and its consequences for the impoverishment of the continent.

If debates on population were so highly speculative, how convincing were the arguments that sought to situate demography at the centre of development? There can be little doubt that by the early fifties overpopulation and Third World poverty were firmly linked together in the Western imagination. An inspection of the pronouncements of politicians and of the popular media shows that by the mid-fifties, the population–development linkage influenced the public mind. However, this influence was primarily the consequence of the force of old-fashioned Western population fears rather than the product of convincing arguments. The more specialist debates of the time show that the thesis that population growth was an obstacle to development lacked any rigorous intellectual foundations. Demographers themselves fluctuated between advocating development as an indirect method of fertility control and promoting population policy as a means for achieving development. Such lack of consistency undermined the case for the population–development linkage.

As one would expect, the population–development linkage was pursued most vigorously by demographers. Others involved in the emerging discipline of development studies were often ready to accept some variant of an overpopulation thesis. Most development specialists were influenced by Western demographic consciousness and ready to conceptualize population as a problem. But in general, their analyses – particularly those of economists – tended to be tentative, even neutral in their pronouncements on the relation between population and development. This was especially the case with those who specialized in the study of underdeveloped societies. A review of the literature indicates that, in particular, the more specialist and the more empirical studies were resistant to the thesis that overpopulation constituted the obstacle to development.

Many of the early pioneers of development studies were strongly influenced by Western demographic consciousness. One of the earliest monographs in what would eventually be known as development studies, Rosenstein-Rodan's 'The international development of economically backward areas', was clearly inspired by this standpoint. Rosenstein-Rodan shared the view that in the colonial regions, economic change would only increase the population without increasing income. In response to what he characterized as the 'population riddle' of the Far East, he proposed the ruthless policy of withholding resources which 'would prevent many people from dying, until sufficient tools, training and equipment was available for the modernisation of these societies'.[21] It is interesting to note that this view, advanced at a lecture to an audience of experts in London in 1944, raised no objections in the discussion that followed. Characteristically, this discussion occurred at a high level of generality, without any consideration of detailed information. Rosenstein-Rodan's main regional expertise was that of Eastern Europe. It was instinct and intuition rather than empirical research into the problems of the Far East that shaped his Malthusian anxieties. It is worth noting that such openly eugenic views were rarely expressed publicly after the end of the war.

4.6 Early Hesitations

Rosenstein-Rodan's strong Malthusian sentiments were rarely echoed by the post-war specialists in the development field. In fact, a small minority of economists actually argued that rather than a problem, population growth was potentially beneficial to the process of development.[22] In some of the early literature, underdevelopment was equated not with a high, but with a low level of population. So, in 1953, the economist Jacob Viner could write that 'a country is often labelled as underdeveloped merely or mainly because it has a low ratio of population to area.'[23] And those specialists who were concerned with 'overpopulation', often conceded that the relation between demographic and developmental trends was far from clear. The absence of any agreement on what constituted this relation is indicated by the comments of some of the most influential development economists.

For instance, Gerald Meier accepted that, as a concept, overpopulation had some relevance. He nevertheless questioned whether it was a cause of underdevelopment. In his 1953 contribution, 'The problem of limited economic development', he observed that 'the problems of increasing capital per head and raising per capita real income are common to all backward economies, whether overpopulated or not.' He added that high levels of population could intensify economic difficulties but not alter their character. Meier concluded that 'overpopulation is simply a manifestation of underdevelopment.'[24]

The connection drawn between overpopulation and underdevelopment was also questioned by Mynt. In an influential article published in 1954, 'The interpretation of economic backwardness', Mynt actually suggested that the 'overpopulation approach' had lost influence and that the discussion was now dominated by the idea of 'underdevelopment'. He argued that while population pressure was in some cases a 'major cause of backwardness', it did 'not explain why other countries not suffering from manifest population pressure should also be similarly backward'. Moreover, he added that in some cases of 'extreme backwardness the size of the backward population has been known to diminish to the point of extinction'.[25]

Neither Meier nor Mynt was in principle opposed to making a connection between population and development. Their doubts and questions were inspired by the information available on the societies of Africa, Asia and Latin America. The argument that there was a causal linkage between population growth and under-development could not be substantiated on the basis of the available information. Even those economists who were drawn towards a Malthusian perspective conceded the difficulty of carrying the argument. Consequently, many specialists substantially qualified the arguments about overpopulation.

The lack of conviction regarding the population–development linkage, was clearly expressed in Arthur Lewis' classic *Theory of Economic Growth* (1965). Lewis accepted the view that population pressure threatened economic well-being, but he refused to treat population pressure as a major cause of underdevelopment. So while he accepted that the 'population problem of some of the poorer countries is very serious' he warned that it was 'not true that population growth, actual or potential, is the principal reason why their levels of living are not rising'. For Lewis, the main culprit was the low rate of capital formation rather than the high rate of population growth. Moreover, empirically it was clear that many poor societies had low population densities. 'Africa is underpopulated, in the sense that the continent still has empty cultivable lands, and in the sense that its present sparse population makes the provision of public utilities very expensive', wrote Lewis (1965, pp. 316, 329). Lewis's insistence that there was no single pattern in the relationship between population and development was echoed by virtually the entire spectrum of development economics. Bauer and Yamey wrote that 'demographic position and trends are not uniform in all under-developed regions'. Simon Kuznets was pessimistic about the very possibility of theorizing the population–development linkage. As far as he was concerned the 'variety of interconnections between population and economic growth' could not be integrated into an adequate theory 'as long as the record and analysis of the diverse population experience of the countries of the world are so incomplete'.[26]

The failure to provide an intellectual rationale for the population–development linkage was not for the lack of trying. Most development specialists a priori accepted some version of the overpopulation thesis, but soon found that their investigation did not always point in that direction. It is a testimony to the integrity of many of these specialists, that they did not allow their assumptions to ignore the unexpected outcome of their research.

Demographers and others devoted to the population problem

were frustrated by the absence of support from the broader intellectual community. The failure to establish a broad Malthusian consensus became evident in the work of the United Nations. There was considerable Western, particularly American, pressure on the United Nations to adopt and promote an unambiguous population control line. However in the fifties it was difficult to gain the backing of international specialists for this project. Discussions revealed a variety of conflicting views and the first major report, *The Determinants and Consequences of Population Trends* was less than clear about the economic effects of population growth.

The report *The Determinants and Consequences of Population Trends* was clearly a product of intellectual compromise. It reviewed the different approaches to the subject and carefully avoided adopting an unambiguous standpoint. It reported that: 'According to some authors, demographic factors seldom if ever exert a very great effect upon economic welfare and progress: according to others they have quite a considerable importance under most conditions and under some conditions rank among the primary factors' (United Nations, 1953, p. 220). This 'on the one hand and on the other' approach ran through the report and infuriated those committed to population control. It certainly showed that proponents of Malthusianism had failed to win the argument.

By the mid-fifties the project of establishing a convincing link between population growth and underdevelopment had reached an intellectual impasse. The strongest proponents of the link were those – such as demographers and journalists – with little specialist knowledge of the societies of the South. They were increasingly impatient with the more specialist academic literature, which was hesitant about taking a clear stand on the issue. Most specialists were prepared intuitively to accept that population was a problem but could not put a case to justify the proposition. Consequently, as the debate on development took off, less and less significance was attached to population.

Those haunted by population fears were conscious of their lack of intellectual authority. Institutions like the Rockefeller Foundation began to finance research into the subject. The most important initiative was the launching of a study into the relation between population growth and economic development at the Office of Population Research, Princeton University in late 1954. Symonds and Carder, in their study *The United Nations and the Population Question*, have emphasized the failure to develop an intellectual foundation for the population–development linkage. In particular they have pointed to the divergence between the outlook of demographers and development specialists: 'Development economists and others involved in the aid programme . . . did not on the whole, come to share the pessimistic outlook of the Malthusian propagandists nor even the more restrained arguments put forward by the demographers until the early sixties' (1973, p. 93). The separation of Malthusian propaganda from serious research helped to limit the impact of population control campaigns. It revealed that population fears were motivated by considerations that had little to do with development. The strength of feeling regarding the economic effects of population growth was not based on serious investigation and analysis. Indeed those who were most involved in research on the subject were precisely the ones least impressed by the claims made on behalf of the population–development linkage.

The intellectual impasse of Malthusian propagandists did not mean that the population–development linkage lacked influence. Through the pronouncements of policy-makers, demographers, journalists and the sensationalism of the popular media, a significant audience was constituted for the view that Third World poverty was the consequence of population pressure. So although population fears could not dominate the development agenda, they still remained a powerful undercurrent. The population control lobby was emotionally convinced that population growth was the crucial obstacle to development and a threat to stability. They were also aware that they now had to find arguments to back their cause. Their attempt to gain intellectual legitimacy will be the subject of the next four chapters.

5

Development and Population Growth

The controversy surrounding the relationship between population growth and its effect on economic development was not resolved during the fifties and sixties. In fact, to this day there is no consensus on the subject. Most contributions, especially those made by economists, accept that the case which links population growth to underdevelopment is not yet proven. But the reluctance of specialists to take a firm stand on this controversy has allowed those convinced of the Malthusian thesis to continue to advocate the population–development linkage. Their intuition, that population growth is a fundamental obstacle to economic development, has prevailed over the conclusions drawn by empirical research. Nevertheless, as this chapter outlines, the attempt to find an economic argument for population control has had to be substantially modified, if not abandoned in favour of other arguments.

Those who support population policy regard the linkage between high rates of fertility and economic stagnation as a self-evident fact. This *a priori* assumption stems from the consciousness of demography, discussed in chapter 1. A review of their literature indicates a cause which is continually in search of good arguments.

The fragile foundation on which the linkage between development and population growth is based is revealed time and again in the literature. Typically, assertions about the negative effects of population growth are often followed by the disclaimer that the connections are far from clear. One well-known textbook, *Popula-*

tion and Development in the Third World, expresses this tendency in the following terms: 'There can be little doubt that rapid population growth has a significant influence in shaping patterns of economic development in the Third World, but many different views have been expressed as to the precise role of population change in the development process (Findlay and Findlay, 1991, p. 41. The absence of a shared view on the role of population does not undermine the conviction – 'there can be little doubt'.

From the standpoint of demographic consciousness, the possibility that there may not be a causal relationship between population and development is seldom entertained. Instead, the procedure adopted is to assume the prior existence of a causal relationship, and then look for proof. Todaro's widely-used textbook on economic development adopts this paradigm (1989, p. 214):

> In recent years economists have begun to focus increasingly on the relationship between economic development and population growth. The most difficult problem for such an analysis, however, is to be able somehow to separate cause from effect. Does economic development accelerate or retard population growth rates or does rapid population growth contribute to or retard economic development? What are the linkages, how strong are they, and in what direction do they operate?

If it is really difficult to separate cause from effect, and if the nature of the linkages are far from clear then why assume in advance that the relationship between population and development is worthy of study? More to the point, why assume that there is even a consistent relationship between the variables? Millions of dollars spent on empirical research have failed to provide convincing support for the view that population growth is an obstacle to development. Nevertheless the conviction that it is so remains undiminished. In this vein, one major review of the literature conceded that economic models have failed to substantiate the population–development link, before stating that 'the absence of a negative correlation' is 'in no sense a criticism of the macro-models under review'. The author's criticism is reserved for those 'who have mistakenly employed the non-correlation argument', that is for those who have dared to question the population–development linkage.[1]

A common substitute for argument and explanation is circular reasoning. In this model, there is a vague and indeterminate but self-evident relationship posited between population and development. For example Teitelbaum, in a paper originally prepared for the Population Council, wrote: 'Population and development are reciprocally and complexly interrelated. Development processes both affect, and are affected by, population variables'.[2] Since just about everything is 'complexly interrelated', it is difficult to challenge Teitelbaum's statement. But statements formulated at such a high level of generality actually indicate a lack of clarity about the subject. Others, too, hide behind the term 'complex', to evade explaining the terms of a relationship that they believe is so important. 'The complexity of the subject makes it tempting to be agnostic about the consequences of rapid population growth', wrote the World Bank in its *World Development Report 1984*. But the Bank clearly avoided this temptation in favour of the conclusion that rapid population growth harmed development (World Bank, 1984, p. 105).

The importance attached to the population–development linkage has gone through a number of distinct changes. During the fifties and sixties, advocates of this linkage were reasonably confident about the validity of their case. However, the argument remained theoretically vulnerable to criticism. A combination of factors – the failure of population programmes, the reaction of Third World people and the growing awareness of the incoherence of the population–development linkage – forced a major rethink in the seventies. The response of the population lobby to its intellectual crisis was quietly to refocus its argument. This shift was never made entirely explicit, but by the seventies the significance attached to the argument that population growth had a negative impact on economic development diminished in importance. And certainly, by the eighties, the arguments that were mobilized to promote population policies were rarely based on the population–development linkage.

The population–development linkage was never explicitly abandoned. Indeed it continues to be used by political figures and journalists. But there can be no doubt that the population lobby has distanced itself from this argument. One important reason why this occurred was because of the force of criticism from many influential economists. As Paul Demeny, a leading intellectual figure associated with the Population Council, wrote recently, 'There was once a strong development rationale for population programs, but the population field became complacent about it and failed to continuously scrutinise and shore up its foundations. When economists mounted an attack on the development rationale, the population field was caught unprepared.'[3] Demeny's acknowledgement of the shift of the population field away from development is in need of minor correction. The population field did not so much fail to continuously scrutinize the problem, as Demeny suggests, but simply lost the argument. This point is acknowledged by Finkle and McIntosh, both insiders in the American population field (1994, pp. 271–2). Nicholas Eberstadt of Harvard University, another vocal supporter of population policies, has indicated his own unease at the tendency to 'shy away from the economic arguments traditionally employed' to justify such policies.[4] This chapter attempts to outline the evolution and resolution of this discussion.

A word of caution. In a world where theoretical themes, policy decisions and political crusading intersect, it is difficult to separate intellectual conviction from tactical compromise. In this chapter, the instrumental character of the debate on population is emphasized; the purpose is to explain and not to condemn. The argument of this chapter is reinforced by the fact that many supporters of the Malthusian cause themselves acknowledge the pragmatic character of their arguments. So Eberstadt has recently remarked on 'a decision by advocates of international population policy to retreat from argumentation in the economic arena'.[5] Hopefully, an analysis of the debate can throw light on why this decision was taken.

5.1 The Coale-Hoover Thesis

The absence of any serious theoretical work on the population–development linkage had become a problem for the population lobby in the fifties. The need to influence key opinion-makers stimulated a demand for new research. The Office of Population Research at Yale University was at the forefront of the response to this demand. The main fruit of this work was Coale and Hoover's *Population Growth and Economic Development in Low-Income Countries*. Published in 1958, Coale and Hoover's work was instantly seized upon as the argument that the population lobby had been waiting for. The Coale-Hoover thesis became highly influential with decision-makers, since it appeared to provide the missing explanation for the population–development linkage. Government reports and academic research regularly cited this work as a vindication of their call for a population policy. According to a well-known account of American population policy, the Coale-

Hoover thesis 'eventually provided the justification for birth control as part of US foreign policy' (Piotrow, 1973, p. 15). According to one account, the Yale demographers made a crucial contribution to the build-up of 'spectacular momentum' behind population policies in the subsequent decade.[6]

So what were the arguments of this influential thesis? Coale and Hoover's case was relatively straightforward. They argued that rapid population growth reduced that share of resources devoted to saving and investment, which in turn had a negative impact on economic growth. From this standpoint, population growth ate up resources and diverted them from productive economic activity. Coale and Hoover identified three areas where population growth had a negative impact on savings and capital accumulation. These were:

1 *Age-dependency effect*. Rapid population growth leads to a high ratio of the economically dependent parts of the population (children) to the productive parts (adults). The consequence of this process is that household income is diverted from savings towards consumption.

2 *Capital-shallowing effect*. Rapid population growth diminishes the ratio of capital to labour. Since capital is spread over a growing number of people, productivity becomes worse than it would have been with a higher ratio of capital to labour.

3 *Investment-diversion effect*. Rapid population growth creates a demand for spending on education and health. These expenditures divert funds from productive investments which would otherwise accelerate the accumulation of capital.

In one form or another these three propositions have been mobilized by advocates of the position that population growth has a negative impact on economic development. The importance of the Coale-Hoover model for strengthening the case for the population–development connection is evident from any review of the literature of the period (see Hawthorn, 1978, p. 2). However, from its inception the Coale-Hoover thesis was always more influential amongst demographers and public officials than among professional economists. Economists and development specialists were often sceptical. With the passing of time, criticisms of this thesis gained momentum so that by the eighties it was virtually abandoned by the mainstream of development studies.

From the outset the Coale-Hoover thesis was challenged on the grounds that it lacked empirical validation. For example, critics pointed out that in Asia some of the most densely settled regions – Singapore, Hong Kong and Taiwan – had the highest output per capita. Others took a more neutral stance but demanded empirical proof for the argument. Tony Thirwall argued that the 'arguments made do not sound unreasonable but they are rarely backed by direct empirical evidence'.[7] Others raised more fundamental issues regarding Coale and Hoover's methodology (see Simon, 1977).

Coale-Hoover's first proposition, the notion of the age-dependency effect, has been dismissed as far too narrow, since the impact of children on household consumption and savings is not at all self-evident. Many families in Asia and Africa are so poor that they possess virtually no savings. In such households the number of children would have little impact on the family's savings. A report published by the World Bank suggested that the bulk of monetized savings is monopolized by a small number of wealthy families. They, in any case 'tend to have few children so their savings are little affected by the burden'. As far as poor families are concerned, would they have more savings if they had fewer children? The report suggested that under such circumstances poor families are likely to consume a 'bit more' rather then save. Another criticism levelled at the age-dependency effect is that poor people may regard their children as not just more mouths to feed but as a way of 'saving' for old age (World Bank, 1984, pp. 82, 83). The very concept of dependency is itself open to question. Many young children actually work in developing societies, and directly contribute to the welfare of the family as a whole. Studies of households in India have shown that children as young as eight years old were productively contributing to the family income (see Michaelson, 1981, p. 112).

Coale and Hoover's second proposition, the concept of the capital-shallowing effect, has also come under question. It has been criticized on the grounds that population growth does not merely dilute the capital available, it may also help the process of accumulation. Allen Kelley has argued that one consequence of rapid population growth is a 'relative abundance of labour *vis-à-vis* capital and land, which raises the returns to these factors and increases the income of their owners'. And since owners of capital and land are likely to be large savers, 'the distribution-of-income effect on saving (and thereby on investment) caused by population growth may offset the forces of capital shallowing.'[8] The highly concentrated character of wealth in developing societies means that savings are not directly influenced by the demographic pattern of average households. Others have argued that economic growth is not reducible to the amount of capital invested – the labour employed can make a decisive contribution to development.

The third proposition, the formulation of the investment-diversion effect, has been criticized too. It has been suggested that this argument – that diverting funds towards unproductive expenditure on education and health slows down growth – underestimates the potential difference which a healthy and educated workforce can make to development. This proposition also begs the question of whether, in the context of a slow-down in the rate of growth of the population, a proportionately greater expenditure for the elderly would be a more productively oriented way of spending societies' resources. The concept of diversion also makes the big assumption that governments would otherwise spend the resources now devoted for the consumption of the young, productively. The record of state investment in most Third World societies indicates that demography is not the only barrier to efficient investment.

Coale and Hoover treat savings as an undifferentiated category. Domestic savings of a society are not the same as personal savings. Personal savings of families only make up a small proportion of domestic savings. The other components are the state and company sectors. It is now generally recognized that the links that Coale and Hoover have drawn between population growth and savings are highly tenuous. For a start, the role of personal savings in the process of capital accumulation is itself far from clear. Some countries, like South Korea, have achieved high rates of economic growth despite low national (personal) saving rates. Many of the agencies which possess substantial savings, such as corporations and governments, are not particularly population sensitive. Consequently, the level of savings is to a considerable extent independent of population growth.

The intellectual foundations of the Coale-Hoover thesis could not for long resist the force of criticism. This is not surprising, since its foundation rested on a recycled Malthusian argument about diminishing returns. Coale and Hoover treated capital in the way that Malthus represented land. It was a fixed quantity that would invariably diminish as the numbers of people increased. In this static model, the 'supply of capital is inelastic' while population is variable. All the way through the analysis, the assumption is that more or less everything is fixed. Consequently, if most factors of production (except for labour) are fixed, changes in population necessarily make a crucial difference. Coale and Hoover argue in this vein: 'Population size has an important if indirect influence on the economic analysis. For example, with a smaller initial population there would be a larger margin of uncultivated land, and more room for increased employment and output in agriculture' (1958, p. 228). Just as land is treated as finite, so the total product of society is treated as a fixed amount. By using up resources, high population growth therefore diminishes the amount that could be divided up between consumers and investors (p. 285).

The Coale-Hoover thesis is so concerned with the problem of consumption that it never considers one of the main obstacles facing developing societies, which is the problem of how to achieve efficient and profitable investment. Savings cannot be invested profitably in many societies which lack the requisite infrastructure and institutional arrangements. Consequently many resource-rich Middle East countries, which possess considerable savings, export their capital to foreign banks. By assuming that the lower the birth rate, the faster the rise in output, Coale and Hoover treat investment as an unproblematic technical matter. From this standpoint individual consumption, rather than the restricted opportunities for profitable investment, becomes the main barrier to economic development. And those resources which are not consumed by a growing population are just there to be invested. That resources are wasted, mismanaged and appropriated for all kinds of non-productive ends is not recognized by this model. Such a simplistic formulation of the relationship between population and investment has now been rejected by virtually everyone involved in theorizing about development. Since the fifties, even those sympathetic to the cause of population control concede that it is not the quantity of investment but the prevailing social relations that influence the dynamic of development.[9]

With hindsight it is evident that the influence of the Coale-Hoover thesis was due to a pre-existing demand for coherent arguments to support population control, rather than to the theoretical depth of the thesis itself. Its influence was most pronounced amongst politicians, public officials and in the popular media. The economic rationale for diminishing returns caught the imagination of the population lobby. For example, in his alarmist account of the 'World Population Problem', Sir Julian Huxley commended the work of the 'two distinguished American economists Asley J. Coale and Edgar M. Hoover'. Huxley reported that 'As regards India they came to the rather drastic conclusion that, if the country did not manage to cut its birth rate by about 50 percent in thirty-five or forty years, it would never be able to develop into a viable industrialised nation; it would reach a point of no return, and its standard of life would go down instead of up.'[10] The main legacy of Coale and Hoover was to provide intellectual confidence for Huxley and other popularizers of the population-explosion theme.

It is important to note that the Coale and Hoover thesis never gained ascendancy amongst professional economists. By the late sixties it was directly questioned by a number of well-known experts in the field of economic development. For example, one of the most authoritative economists dealing with population questions, Simon Kuznets, queried whether there was any relationship between population growth and levels of living standards. Kuznets was not unsympathetic to the policy of population control, but he believed that this was a relatively insignificant issue compared to the more profound obstacle posed by the institutions of developing societies. Similarly, the British economist Tony Thirwall was prepared to accept that 'curbing population growth may be desirable', but not because it undermined living standards. 'The relationship between population growth and living standards is largely inconclusive', he wrote. By the early seventies, the Coale and Hoover thesis was abandoned even by committed proponents of population control. For example, Robert Cassen could dismiss the 'small number of relatively crude ideas' which dominated the work of economists. The crude ideas he had in mind sounded suspiciously like the previously acclaimed Coale-Hoover thesis.[11]

The different responses to the Coale and Hoover thesis from development specialists and policy-makers, were characteristic of the evolution of the debate. Clearly demographic consciousness continued to exercise considerable influence regardless of the conclusions drawn by empirical research. This lack of regard for the evidence should not be understood as a consequence of dishonesty and manipulation. It is a testimony to the strength of the conviction that the growth of population represented the fundamental problem.

5.2 The Battle over the Population Agenda

The reservations expressed by development economists about the population–development linkage rarely intruded into the public domain. At the level of policy-making, there was a disposition to accept the population–development linkage, regardless of the outcome of theoretical debates. Political anxieties about overpopulation far outweighed the findings of academic debate. That is why, in the United States and to a lesser extent in other Western societies, the population lobby found it relatively easy to influence government officials. By the late fifties the view that overpopulation was primarily responsible for Third World poverty and for the consequent instability was widely accepted in official circles. It was only a matter of time before population control would be projected into the sphere of foreign policy, as the obvious answer to the problems of underdevelopment and instability.

During the fifties and sixties, in the United States, a number of population pressure groups and major foundations were involved in winning over public opinion and officialdom to the cause of population control. They were also involved in scientific research on forms of contraception that could be used in the implementation of population programmes in Third World societies. With the invention of cheap forms of contraceptives, population control appeared as a viable policy option. During the sixties, leading American officials initiated a crusade for population control. The argument deployed was simple and to the point: since population growth was the major obstacle to development, the control of fertility was the obvious solution to the problem. International officials at the time even argued that funds spent on population programmes were better value for money than investments on development projects. In a highly publicized speech, Robert McNamara, the head of the World Bank told his audience at Notre Dame University in May 1969: 'Family Planning programs are less costly than conventional development projects, and the pattern of expenditures involved is normally very different. At the same time, we are conscious of the fact that successful programs of this kind will yield very high economic results' (cited in Mass, 1976, p. 61).

This argument gained momentum and came to constitute the dominant outlook of American officialdom. This had far-reaching consequences. The American government not only ended up officially endorsing population control, it also succeeded in converting international agencies like the World Bank and the UN to support this perspective. In turn, agencies like the World Bank took a lead in selling population policies to Third World governments.

During the sixties, population policy emerged as an integral part of development ideology. It is difficult to untangle what exactly motivated official agencies to support population control. Some have suggested that it was the fear of the West losing access to natural resources, some have pointed to anxiety about instability, whilst others have pointed to the alarm that was expressed about apparent food shortages. In addition, some radical critics have pointed to the motif of racism and the exigencies of imperialist control (for conflicting views and emphasis see Piotrow, 1973; P. J. Donaldson, 1990; and Mass, 1976). Whatever the motives, the speed with which the policy of population control gained ascendancy was truly remarkable. The reservations that were expressed about the economic role of population in the specialist literature were seldom acknowledged in public statements. This was a one-sided public discussion. That is why, at the time, the new policy barely provoked any opposition in the West. Until the eighties, there was virtually no domestic opposition to America's overseas family planning programme.

Many officials were carried away by their enthusiasm for the policy of population control. As with the population–development linkage, the belief in the effectiveness of this policy had the character of blind faith. From the start, the argument rested on the unproven assumption that a reduction in the rate of fertility would stimulate economic growth. It then concluded that the best way for reducing the rate of fertility was to provide contraception and family planning services. The assumption behind this proposal was that there already existed a huge demand for birth control in developing societies. Consequently, it was suggested that there would be a ready-made demand for population policies. As Donald Warwick, who was commissioned to evaluate family planning programmes by the United Nations Fund for Population Activities (UNFPA), argued, it was believed that irrespective of socio-economic and cultural circumstances, all women of reproductive age wanted to limit their fertility. This assumption of universal demand was explicitly formulated in 1966, by the Population Council in the following terms (cited in Warwick, 1987,

p. 34): 'It is often argued that in the traditional societies people are not really ready for or interested in family planning. The experience of the council is that people are amazingly ready and that the difficulty lies in the failure of governmental personnel to realise that fact'.[11] It was assumed that once women were acquainted with the virtues of contraceptive technology, they would instantly seize the opportunity to practise birth control. That there were strong cultural and socio-economic factors influencing decisions about fertility was not seriously considered.

The dogmatic rationale for population policy was most striking in the sphere of survey research. At the time it was fashionable to mount surveys to measure the prevailing motivation for limiting fertility in Third World societies. These initiatives, called the Knowledge-Attitude-Practice (KAP) surveys, were designed to measure the degree of demand for family planning. But because they were mounted by agencies interested in promoting population control policies, KAP services tended merely to affirm the existence of widespread demand. As Warwick argued, these were not just surveys, but surveys designed to sell a product (1982, p. 35).[12] Consequently, the surveys had the character of an exercise in public relations. Bernard Berelson, former head of the Population Council explained the purpose of the KAP surveys in the following terms: 'A survey should probably be done at the outset of any national program – partly for its evaluational . . . use but also for its political use, in demonstrating to the elite that the people themselves strongly support the program and in demonstrating to the society at large that family planning is generally approved' (cited in Hartmann, 1987, pp. 58–9). The surveys were not so much investigations as demonstrations of an *a priori* position.

Advocates of population policy were always happy to believe the conclusions of these surveys. For example the Pearson Report, *Partners in Development* (1969), was absolutely convinced that it was merely a question of getting the contraceptive pills into the right hands. 'Numerous field surveys of parents in developing countries indicate that birth rates would be reduced by one-third if parents had the knowledge and means to plan the size of their families', was its verdict (p. 57).

It was not too long before the assumption of universal demand for birth control was exposed as wishful thinking. Numerous initiatives, which were launched in the sixties, were disoriented by the difficulties they experienced in implementing family planning programmes. Such programmes, which were entirely donor–

driven, failed to display sensitivity to the local circumstances within which they operated. Sometimes, as in India, the frustration with lack of progress led to the use of coercive methods which in turned provoked resistance. More often, they were just ineffective. Campaigns, for example in India, Egypt and Kenya failed to realize their objective of lowering the birth rate. Experience indicated that the policy of population control was less than effective. As Warwick argued: 'By 1970 it was clear that family planning supply was running well ahead of demand. Whereas 60 or 70 per cent of eligible women might report in a survey that they were interested in limiting births, when they were provided with the services the majority did not use them' (1987, p. 3). Clearly the time had come for a major reassessment of family planning programmes. This reassessment was also necessitated by the emergence of vocal criticism of population policies.

The apparent failure of population policies called into question the assumption of universal demand. Doubts about the existence of universal demand for contraception also coincided with the growth of opposition to Western population policies. During the early seventies, the relationship between population and development was placed under scrutiny. Some criticized population control on the grounds that it was a poor substitute for development. Others suggested that the emphasis on population diverted attention from the real problem of development. And radical critics took the view that the demand for reducing the numbers of Third World people served only the interest of Western domination.

The growing influence of anti-Malthusian sentiments in the Third World took the population lobby in the West unawares. Until the early seventies, it was assumed that the main barrier facing population policy in the Third World was indifference rather than active hostility. But the emergence of a Third World bloc demanding a new economic deal created an entirely unexpected situation. Western population policies became caught up in the North–South debate about the future of the world. A review of this debate noted at the time, that 'the near identity between high fertility and low development status' meant 'that international discussions of population have increasingly taken on the flavour of a debate between the developing and developed worlds, in the same category as such debates regarding raw materials, colonialism, and the terms of international trade'.[13]

The controversy regarding population control came to a head at the World Population Conference in Bucharest in August 1974. For the population lobby, the holding of an international conference on population, represented the culmination of a successful international promotion campaign. In the previous decade, resolutions passed by a number of United Nations agencies had the effect of establishing family planning as a 'human right'. It was expected that the Bucharest conference would provide further legitimacy and thus boost the cause of population control. However, the conference was overtaken by other discussions, in particular the North–South controversy about the distribution of the world's resources. Many Third World critics argued against the view that population growth was 'the' problem. They sought to win support for the principle 'that population problems are not a cause but a consequence of underdevelopment – and the most effective solution for underdevelopment is a New International Order'.[14] Because of international political considerations, this so-called developmentalist perspective could not be ignored and the final resolution of the Bucharest Conference toned down the previous one-dimensional emphasis on population programmes.

The debate at Bucharest was important, because it indicated that population policies had become politicized and could no longer be treated as mere technical concerns. It also helped bring the intellectual crisis of the population lobby to the surface. Many accounts of the debate in the seventies emphasize the theme of the difference of views between North and South. But there were other important forces at work leading to the recasting of population arguments. By the time that the Bucharest conference was held, there were serious questions raised about the effectiveness of population programmes even amongst their advocates. As indicated earlier, the experience suggested that such policies were difficult to implement. In many underdeveloped societies, the prevailing socio-economic conditions were not favourable to population programmes. The contradiction between socio-economic realities and the aspirations of the population lobby had become apparent to many observers. As Finkle and Crane reported in their interesting review of the Bucharest conference; 'the contention that fertility decline cannot take place without prior economic development was further buttressed by the apparent lack of success of many countries with family planning programmes.'[15] Those who advocated an autonomous population policy and minimized the relevance of social change were put on the defensive at Bucharest. They were particularly taken aback when John D. Rockefeller III, one of the leading figures in the American lobby for population control, openly argued that population programmes had to be linked to a developmental strategy. 'We recognise that reducing population growth is not an alternative to development, but an essential part of it for most countries' (cited in Mass, 1976, p. 68). Rockefeller's change of tack anticipated the new approach of the population lobby.

Many observers have argued that it was at Bucharest that population policies acquired a developmentalist form. Bonnie Mass has cast serious doubts on this conclusion. She noted that after Bucharest 'the population programs of the future would have to be couched in more subtle terminology.' And she added that in order to be 'palatable to recipient countries, population control programs would have to be more developmentalist in approach' (1976, p. 105). According to Mass, this was a tactical compromise rather than a fundamental revision of objectives. Terms like population control and even population policy had to give way to more acceptable developmentalist ones. Mass's instinct was to be borne out by subsequent events. This was an empty rhetoric with little developmental content.

As an aside it is worth noting that the consensus arrived at in Bucharest did not match the whole-hearted developmentalist perspective of the demographers of the forties and fifties. As we shall see, the central significance previously assigned to 'rapid economic growth' was quietly abandoned in favour of other arguments. As most accounts of the history of this debate reveal, the population lobby never felt comfortable with the developmental consensus of Bucharest. In such accounts, terms like 'malaise', loss of a 'sense of direction' and of crisis of 'confidence', testify to the lack of conviction behind this reorientation.[16]

5.3 The Post-Bucharest Consensus

The politicization of the issue of population at Bucharest had the effect of widening the debate. There were important political and intellectual issues at stake and the exigencies of diplomacy demanded that population policy be recast in a developmentalist framework. At the same time, many supporters of population policies were conscious of the weakness of the intellectual underpinnings of their arguments. The outcome of these pressures was a major rethink.

In the light of the experience with population programmes, even dedicated supporters began to question some of the underlying assumptions. In 1975, Paul Demeny of the Population Council suggested that the failure of population programmes might be due to the fact that they were not needed (see P. J. Donaldson, 1990, p. 56). Others argued that the decision by poor families to have a large number of children was based on a rational calculation about the needs of people in impoverished societies. This revision of the previous assumption of universal demand for family planning implicitly represented a rejection of the ideas associated with the Coale-Hoover model. If the decisions made about the size of the family were perceived as motivated by rational calculations, then the individualistic orientation of family planning would be called into question. This insight helped redirect research towards an examination of attitudes towards fertility at the level of the household. This research soon revealed that many poor families attached a positive value to large families and regarded their children as a positive asset.[17] As socio-economic and cultural factors came into the picture, the view that population growth was by definition problematic, could no longer be sustained.

Those concerned with upholding population policies were forced to come up with more acceptable arguments. The seventies saw a ceaseless search for new ammunition for the Malthusian cause. This was a period of intellectual compromise and pragmatism, but also of innovation. In retrospect, proponents of population policy see this period as one where their movement lacked confidence and lost its direction. In their account of the movement's history, McIntosh and Finkle have observed that the view that 'rapid population growth is an obstacle to development was probably at its peak' in the fifties and sixties. They give four reasons for the setback experienced by the population lobby in the seventies. They first point to the strong reactions in Third World societies, provoked by the insensitive 'military campaign' that characterized many population programmes. In passing they also concede that the contraceptive technology deployed 'undoubtedly violated many ethical principles that have since been recognised'. Secondly they note that the 'attack mounted by a coalition of third world countries' at Bucharest was the 'most critical factor undermining the confidence of the population establishment'. Thirdly, they observe that there was a 'growing recognition that the widespread distribution of contraceptives was insufficient by itself to motivate women to accept them'. And finally they concede that the 'views of economists who were questioning the underlying assumption that population growth is inimical to economic development were also important' (Finkle and McIntosh, 1994, pp. 272–3).

McIntosh and Finkle, who are broadly sympathetic to the cause of the population establishment, characterise the post-Bucharest consensus as representing a new rationale for 'organised family planning programmes'. Having lost the argument for an economic rationale for fertility control, the population lobby had to look for new ideas. McIntosh and Finkle note, that 'several years were required for the population establishment to regroup after these attacks on its basic tenets.'

The Bucharest compromise was reflected in the population literature. The case for population programmes was now presented in a more subtle fashion. Population growth was rarely presented as the fundamental problem. Instead it was now treated as one important variable in the underdevelopment equation. In this way the population–development linkage was retained, if in a compromised form, and in many contributions a diminished economic role was now assigned to population growth. According to the World Bank, population growth was not 'unimportant', but it was 'only one influence, among many others, on any variable in an economic system' (1974, p. 25). Cassen's compromise formulation was distinctly defensive in tone. He stated that the influence of population on economic growth was 'relatively small in comparison with other influences' or 'at the very least' it was 'not big enough to dominate everything else'.[18] This more modest defence of the population–development linkage gradually supplanted the more ambitious claims of Coale-Hoover. In light of the debate at Bucharest, Todaro conceded that 'population growth is not the only, or even the primary, source of low levels of living' in the Third World (1989, p. 202).

During the mid-seventies, the economic justification for population policy was compromised. As Mark Perlman argued in 1975, in his review of the discussion of the relationship between population and economic growth, 'if we use anti-natalist programs, we do so for reasons other than those simply offered by what we as economists now know.'[19] Increasingly, economic growth was used less and less as the main rationale for population programmes.

In passing, it is worth noting that during the early eighties, the thesis that population growth acted as an obstacle to economic growth came under further attack. This period saw the ascendancy of liberal free-market economics, which regarded all forms of state intervention with suspicion. American monetarists were keen to demonstrate that Third World poverty was the legacy of state intervention in the market. From this perspective, population programmes were merely another variant of market interference. During Ronald Reagan's presidency in the eighties, economists who were agnostic or even critical about the desirability of population programmes received a boost. Official agencies and even international institutions like the World Bank became less enthusiastic, or at least more circumspect, about promoting population policies. For example an influential report, published in 1986 by the National Research Council, conceded that there was 'no statistical association between national rates of population growth and growth rates of income per capita' (p. 4). Even the World Bank (1984) adopted a more hesitant position on this question.

The swift acceptance of the view that population was not the main barrier to development illustrates the superficial character of the Bucharest developmentalist framework. It is probably more accurate to describe this process as one where development was redefined to mean all things to all people. Consequently, the distancing of population programmes from economic growth did not mean that the population–development linkage was entirely abandoned. A process of reflection and redefinition ensued. As Perlman indicated, new arguments needed to be elaborated to uphold support for population policies. Some of these arguments stressed the contribution that population programmes could make to public health and to the position of women and children. Other arguments emphasized issues such as the problem of the environment and of food production – themes which will be discussed in the next three chapters.

An interesting paradox is evident in the post-Bucharest discussion. The new emphasis on development, which emerged as part of the consensus of the mid-seventies, had largely the character of a compromise. But this was not apparent to many observers at the time, because the Bucharest consensus was interpreted as a major concession to the developmental aspirations of Third World societies. And indeed, at the level of tactics and rhetoric, it did represent a concession. Consequently, the acceptance of the Bucharest developmental vocabulary obscured the new direction of the population lobby.

In reality, the new consensus shifted the focus away from the theme of economic development and growth. It is difficult to find any serious contribution published in the past fifteen years, which justifies population control on the grounds that population increase is the obstacle to economic growth.[20] This is clearly reflected in the switch from macroeconomic concern with growth rates to the more influential microeconomic studies concerned with the effects of fertility decline.

5.4 The Quiet Shift from Development

Economic growth has been increasingly replaced by redistribution as a central motif in the population literature. A new linkage between population and redistribution was formulated in the seventies, to replace the previous one between economic growth and fertility. Rapid population growth was now presented as a problem for the distribution of income, rather than as an obstacle to the rise of per capita income. Cassen for example accepted that it was 'hard to substantiate the view of Third World poverty as caused in any way by population growth' whilst arguing that there was a tendency for 'income distribution to worsen under common patterns of high fertility'.[21] The World Bank argued an identical position: 'whereas some people regard the effect of reduced fertility on per capita income growth as ambiguous, there appears to be no explicit dissent from the view that lower fertility contributes to greater income equality' (1974, p. 35). So while the National Research Council took an agnostic position on the relationship between economic and population growth, it accepted that family planning programmes could 'help to advance equity goals' (1986, p. 92). This redistributionist orientation evolved in a number of different directions. Some emphasized the improvement to the overall quality of life and health, while others pointed to the benefits to women that a population policy would bring.

The new consensus recast population programmes as a policy of reform. According to the new wisdom, the reduction of poverty provided the motive for families to reduce their size. Population policy, in its redistributionist form, appeared more radical than previously. After the experience of Bucharest, and the strong reaction from nationalist Third World Governments, the population lobby self-consciously adopted a more radical tone. Demographic research was explicitly directed towards the issues of poverty and equity.[22] Cassen even invited Marxists and radicals to join the new consensus. 'A radical examination of questions of environmental pollution, use of exhaustible resources, or labour force and capital growth in development would all be welcome, as would be Marxist sociological analyses of fertility, or of the social and political consequences of population growth', he wrote.[23]

Many critics of the more coercive policies of population control were drawn to the new approach, which promoted the quality of life and attacked inequalities. Even the literature critical of population policy regarded the new consensus as a step in a positive direction. They perceived the shift from one-dimensional population policy to broader socio-economic concerns as a step in the right direction. Bondestam and Bergstrom took the view that the Bucharest consensus helped reorient the discussion towards wider developmental issues. According to them, this discussion of wider issues, constituted 'a step in a less biased direction' (1980, pp. vii–viii). This was also the view of Erland Hofsten, who looked upon the Bucharest consensus as an affirmation of the principle of development (Bondestam and Bergstrom, 1980, p. 218). Even Betsy Hartmann, one of the most trenchant critics of mainstream population policy, recorded that Bucharest represented a positive step. She wrote that the seventies were a 'time of soul searching about the meaning and purpose of development'. According to Hartmann, the 'acknowledgement of the population–development linkage was a big step forward' (1987, pp. 108–9). This reaction was understandable, as the focus of the literature on Third World population issues shifted to adopt the language of equity and redistribution.

Throughout most of the literature, the post-Bucharest consensus is characterized as a developmentalist one. But closer inspection of the discussion suggests a fundamentally different interpretation of the evolution of the narratives of demography. What happened was that redistribution replaced economic growth as the justification for population policy. But the concern with population remained – only the argument for population policy changed. Indeed, the importance attached to redistribution was precisely that it curbed population growth. No doubt many specialists were genuinely attracted to the new egalitarian message. However, this attachment to redistribution was as instrumental as the previous focus on economic growth. Todaro argued the case for redistribution in the following way:

> Our conclusion, therefore, is that it is not so much the *aggregate* level of per capita income that matters for population growth but rather how that income is *distributed*. The social and economic institutions of a

nation and its philosophy of development are probably greater determinants of population growth rates than are aggregate economic variables and simplistic models of macroeconomic growth (1989, p. 220).

Todaro's concern was neither with the level of per capita income
nor with its distribution. His aim was to isolate the variable that has
the most direct influence on the rate of fertility. And the significance attached to income distribution was to do with its apparent
influence on the rate of growth of fertility. Distribution of income
was and continues to be promoted as a means for achieving
demographic objectives. As Ronald Ridker argued; 'all the evidence, statistical and historical, gathered both within and among
countries, points in the same direction: the distribution of income
appears to have an impact on fertility, one that ought to be
amenable to policy manipulation.'[24]

Although the new consensus was presented in a developmentalist
vocabulary, its aim was the old objective of effectively curbing the
rate of fertility. Through the redefinition of the problem, the
meaning of development was transformed. It was no longer about
growth, increasing output or technological change – it was about
how existing resources were to be shared out. Thus the new
consensus at least implicitly represented an abandonment of the
search for intellectual justification for the population–development linkage. Unfortunately, at the time, this was rarely openly
acknowledged. And in contrast to the specialist literature, journalistic contributions on the subject, still often argue the case that
population growth harms development. Despite the changing
emphasis of the specialist literature, the assumption that there is
some linkage between population and development continued to
survive.

One consequence of the new consensus was that at the level of
theory, the previously accepted relationship between fertility transition and economic development was substantially modified.
Increasingly, it was suggested that fertility transition could take
place without economic development or that only a specific type of
development influenced population growth. This point is now
openly argued by a number of experts. For example Bengsston and
Gunnarsson question the old Bucharest consensus that 'socio-
economic development is the best contraceptive' by stating that
'security is the best contraceptive.'[25] Since economic development
need not be a precondition for security, the connection between
demographic patterns and socio-economic change is severed. At

the level of theory, this separation of demographic pattern from socio-economic change was reflected in the growing disenchantment of the population lobby with the theory of demographic transition.

Those most committed to population control have always believed that development was something of a diversion from their fundamental concern and that contraception was the best means of contraception. They were never reconciled to the Bucharest position that 'development is the best pill.' Many commentators consider that these two positions are directly antithetical to each other. To be sure, there is an important difference of emphasis. But the two approaches share the common assumption that some kind of 'pill' is needed to deal with the prior problem of population growth. In one case the solution is the contraceptive pill, in another it is a wider and more indirect policy of change. It can be argued that these differences are tactical rather then strategic. In reality these alternatives are not mutually contradictory. Direct and indirect approaches to fertility control are not necessarily antithetical to each other. As indicated in the previous chapter, the same demographers have promoted one or the other at different times. Controversy about the means obscures a surprising degree of agreement about fundamentals.

The quiet abandonment of the attempt to construct a conceptual connection between development and population did not imply any reduction of interest in demographic issues. Indeed since the eighties, interest in the issue of Third World population has grown enormously. However, this interest is rarely expressed in traditional developmental terms. As the introduction to a recently published text on the subject noted, this interest is 'largely fuelled by ecological concerns' (Lutz, 1994, p. xiv). And many environmentalists devoted to population control regard economists with their developmental interests as hostile opponents. The well-known environmentalist, Lester Brown, has argued that 'nowhere is the conceptual contrast between economists and ecologists more evident than in the way they view population growth' (1991, p. 15). There is no room for economic development in Brown's biological model. And his preferred environmental themes do not exhaust the new arguments made on behalf of population control. It is to the new concerns, and to the new arguments on behalf of population control, that we now turn.

6

Influencing Fertility: Modernization without Development

Since the early eighties, the population lobby has redirected the focus of its propaganda away from development. In the discussion of fertility control, far less significance is now attached to economic growth than was the case in the immediate post-war decades. Many advocates of population programmes strongly reject the old orthodoxy which associated economic development with the stabilization of population growth. They contend that economic development does not necessarily lead to a reduction in the rate of fertility. They also argue that attitudes towards family size can be influenced outside the context of development and that population control objectives can be realized without the need for far-reaching social change. This perspective of influencing attitudes towards fertility promotes a process which can be called modernization without development. It is a perspective based on the premise that those attitudes towards fertility which generally prevail in industrialized societies can be paralleled in the South prior to development.

The more fervent Malthusians, with a strong sense of natural limits, were always suspicious of development. The Ehrlichs, for example, regarded economic growth as having undesirable consequences for the environment. They were also critical of the growth orientation of professional economists for ignoring the so-called 'realities of geology and biology'. In place of economic growth, the Ehrlichs advocated the policy of 'semi-development' for the Third World. This was a policy which eschewed industrialization and growth in favour of agrarian self-sufficiency (1970, pp. 280, 303–7). Most advocates of population policy did not go as far as the Ehrlichs in directly rejecting development. As indicated in the previous chapter, the general tendency was to modify the meaning of development to mean redistribution.

The shift from development to redistribution was motivated by a number of influences. Some of these influences emerged independently of the field of demography. The most important was the widely acknowledged 'crisis ' in development thinking in the seventies. The failure of traditional development policy in the seventies created a general climate of scepticism towards this project. Cumulative economic growth appeared as an elusive goal for most industrializing societies. The recognition that development strategy had reached an impasse coincided with an explosion of environmental consciousness in the West. The lack of belief in growth models along with an influential stream of anti-growth sentiment played an important role in encouraging the emerging redistributionist consensus within the field of demography. Even stridently growth oriented institutions like the World Bank changed their vocabulary and pragmatically adopted the language of sustainable development.

The movement towards the perspective of redistribution was also very much a response to mounting opposition to and criticism of the record of population policies. The previous one-dimensional emphasis on population control and direct methods of birth control was controversial and provoked widespread hostility in the Third World. The direct stress on reducing numbers exposed the population community to widespread criticism. Redistributive policies were part of a reorientation from these direct methods to the indirect approach to achieving fertility decline. An important component of this shift was a greater stress on propaganda and public relations. As Findlay and Findlay argue 'marketing has become as important as medicine in promoting birth control' (1991, p. 67). Many believed that it was easier to sell family planning as part of a wider redistributive package than as a programme explicitly designed to stabilize numbers.

For the purposes of this discussion, it is important not to exaggerate the significance of the shift from development to redistribution. The commitment of the population lobby to development was always an instrumental one – development was a means to the end of fertility control. The new advocacy of redistribution represented a shift in rationale for justifying the same objective of population control. Redistribution was valued because it was seen as a more effective contraceptive then development. Proponents of this position believed that it was more effective because it touched more people then development. To some extent this response was influenced by the many problems encountered by developing societies. Economic growth was concentrated in a few parts of developing societies and did not appear to have the effect of changing a lot of people's lives. Some argued that economic growth influenced only the fertility behaviour of the small group who benefited from economic growth: 'It is now evident, however, that because of unequal distribution of wealth, economic development in poorer countries does not necessarily lower the overall birth rate. Rather, it results in lowered birth rates for the small minority who amass personal wealth'.[1] This pessimistic account of the effects of economic development on the rate of fertility continues to be argued by many in the population field. From their standpoint, the merit of redistribution is that it reaches a far larger section of society. For example, a mass education campaign can reach even those who are marginal to the process of economic development.

In passing, it should be noted that the term redistribution as used by population publicists has no precise meaning. It does not always imply a redistribution of society's resources to its people. It is often used in a pragmatic sense to mean the provision of certain services, particularly education, to wide sections of society.

The shift in paradigm from growth to redistribution was often a superficial one. Often it involved little more than the substitution of terms – whereas before it was development, now it was redistribution which was said to be the answer. Robert Repetto's *Economic Equality and Fertility in Developing Countries* (1979) provided a classic account of the redistributionist standpoint. The central thesis of Repetto was that it was not so much underdevelopment but economic inequality that was responsible for high rates of fertility growth. Repetto claimed that, 'for a community at any level of economic development, as measured by *average* income per capita or some similar index, the overall birth rate of the community will be lower, the more equally distributed that total income is.' According to Repetto, inequality boosted population growth because if resources were monopolized by a small elite, any decline in fertility would be concentrated in a small section of society. The vast majority of an economically marginalized population, living an insecure existence would inevitably display an orientation towards high rates of fertility. Repetto argued for redistribution on the grounds that different patterns of income distribution led to different rates of population growth. He also contended that redistribution made a positive contribution to not only population control, but also to development. Redistribution leading to a lower rate of population growth permitted a faster accumulation of capital per worker, which in turn led to a faster increase in output per worker (pp. 1–5). So in a round-about way, redistribution achieved some of the objectives previously assigned to rapid economic growth.

Since the early eighties, redistributionist writers have stressed the importance of the link between poverty and a regime of high fertility. This was one of the main propositions of the 1984 World Bank Report. The Report commented that 'rapid population growth is associated at household and national levels, with slower progress in raising living standards, especially of the poor' (p. 184). This report like other contributions on the subject regarded poverty as expressive of a culture of high fertility. 'When poverty persists, traditional patterns of organization persist and so do traditional forms of fertility behaviour', wrote Bengtsson and Gunnarsson. Many experts believe that the condition of poverty generates a way of life where high fertility becomes a self-perpetuating process. Nancy Birdsall wrote that 'poverty is both a root cause and a common outcome of high fertility'. Birdsall suggested that a number of significant characteristics of poor households could contribute to high fertility: 'high infant mortality, lack of education for women, too little family income to "invest" in children, leading to parents having many children rather than concentrating investments in a few, and finally, for many poor couples, poor access to contraception of reasonable cost and quality'.[2] Another variant of this argument suggests that the poor calculate that large numbers of children make life easier to survive. Ndalahwa Madulu argues that in Tanzania, it is the poor living conditions in rural areas which 'stimulate a greater demand for large families'.[3]

The Brutland Commission Report, *Our Common Future* (World Commission on Environment and Development, 1987), reaffirmed the proposition that poverty was associated with the culture of high fertility. 'Poverty breeds high rates of population growth', it reported, adding that 'almost any activity that increases well-being and security lessens people's desires to have more children than they and the national ecosystem can support' (pp. 98 and 106). Poverty was targeted because of the conviction that this would be the most effective antidote to the culture of high fertility. This raises an interesting paradox. The targeting of poverty was elaborated as an alternative to the population–development linkage. However, any amelioration in the lives of the masses of poor people presupposes some degree of development. Redistribution without development can have only a superficial impact on people's lives. This is ignored by the advocates of redistribution. Consequently, the various reports on poverty often have an abstract quality. For example, a report published by the United Nations, *World Population: Trends and Policies* (1988), observed in passing how 'adverse economic trends' made it difficult for 'many Governments to implement effectively policies aimed at improving social and economic welfare, including population policies' (p. 11). Nevertheless, the report continued to discuss redistributionist policy options, as if they were intrinsically viable regardless of economic circumstances. In effect, poverty was abstracted from its social context and treated as the unfortunate consequence of maldistribution. This procedure continues to be followed in the population literature, where poverty is often treated as an independent variable responsible for high rates of fertility.

The policies that are proposed by redistributionists help shed some light on their underlying concern with poverty. These policies have no potential for eliminating poverty, for the very simple reason that in the absence of socio-economic change there are no viable anti-poverty policies. Rather, the aim of the redistributionist policies is to eliminate the culture of high fertility that is associated with poverty. In most cases redistribution becomes merely the means of influencing the pattern of fertility among poor people, to counter traditional practices.

Paradoxically, policies which seek to eliminate 'traditional' practices have always been a dominant theme in Western development theory. In the mainstream Western literature development was equated with modernization. And modernization was generally defined as the historical and social processes which the West had experienced. Hence the term modernization was used interchangeably with Westernization. Modernization theory argued that progress in the Third World depended on the elimination of traditional values and practices. It advocated the promotion of a more individualistic lifestyle, including the adoption of the Western nuclear family system (see Worsley, 1987, p. 67). The similarity of this approach with the redistributionist thesis is striking. In both cases, the objective is to replace traditional attitudes with Western ones. But whereas modernization theory posited this objective in the context of economic development, the redistributionist perspective is restricted to influencing attitudes – specifically attitudes to family size. Hence the redistributionist perspective can be understood as that of modernization without development.

The main aim of redistributionist policies is to encourage family nucleation. Many demographers believe that institutionalizing the nuclear family is the prerequisite for fertility decline in the Third World. The aim of population policy is to challenge attitudes and practices which act as a barrier to the nucleation of the family. In some cases, this represents an undeclared war on traditions which are inhospitable to individualistic behaviour. Agnes Riedmann has argued that population policies in Nigeria were 'cultural impositions' which sought to win adherents to the view that the 'real' family was nuclear. Research workers involved in a survey were implicitly challenging 'taken-for-granted assumptions of Yoruba life'. Riedmann observed that those involved in the survey offered 'representations of public morality in support of purposefully limited family size' (1993, pp. 68–9 and 78). Riedmann's work on Nigeria raises some important issues about the enterprise of challenging cultural values and practices. At what point does the attempt to target fertility behaviour become propaganda or even a form of alien imposition?

Most population activists believe that the worthiness of their cause entitles them to change the attitudes and norms of 'traditional' people. They are also convinced that the attitude of the poor peasant is there to be changed. Some have boasted that even without any economic advance, traditional values can be transformed. 'Even in poor countries that were relatively untouched by development, new attitudes have taken root, and more couples are having smaller families.'[4] Some of the policies proposed to realize this objective are: raising rural incomes, educating parents, especially women, improving the status of women, reducing infant mortality and the provision of family planning services.

Demographers believe that all the policies mentioned above contribute towards the containment of fertility growth. However, some of these policies are easier to put into practice than others. Real redistribution, such as increasing the income of the rural poor is extremely difficult to implement and is rarely acted on. In comparison the mounting of a family planning programme is relatively straightforward. Most often redistribution actually means nothing more then the implementation of family planning programmes. The most common form of 'redistribution' is the provision of contraceptive technology for the poor. After listing the different policies available for influencing fertility, a United Nations report conceded that 'among these measures, the establishment, expansion or strengthening of family planning services has been most widely used' (1988, p. 14). The gap that separates the rhetoric of redistribution from the policies pursued, testifies to the abstract character of the discussion of poverty. The discussion on poverty has the character of a preamble – which is quietly ignored when policy options are practically considered.

The themes of equity and welfare endow redistributive population policies with an enlightened image. Those who uphold this perspective sometimes even evoke so-called socialist countries like Cuba and China as proof that redistributionist policies work to stabilize fertility. The association of population policy with a more equitable society gives it a progressive image. Thus radical critics of the unequal world system feel comfortable with the approach. In this way high fertility is assimilated into a spectrum of problems which range from inequality to oppression. So Frances Moore Lappé and Rachel Schurman argue: 'We find it most fruitful to view the varied forces keeping birth rates high as aspects of a systematic denial of essential human rights – understood to include not only political liberties, but access to life-sustaining resources and to educational and economic opportunity' (1989, p. 68). Large families, which are traditionally condemned by Malthusians, are here problematized as an expression of lack of rights. From this perspective, birth control is reinterpreted as primarily an anti-poverty and pro-human rights issue. Advocates of the human rights thesis rarely consider the deeper implications of their arguments. For example people may well choose to exercise their right to have lots of children. To represent high birth rates as a symptom of lack of rights is to assume that if people possessed 'essential human rights' they would always choose to have small families. Such conclusions are not warranted from the available evidence.

Amongst radical proponents of redistribution, an equitable society is often sharply counterposed to growth and development. Asoka Bandrage wrote that 'what is most essential for poverty alleviation and declining birth rates is not overall economic growth but rather equitable income distribution, the reduction of economic inequality, and improvements in women's lives.'[5] Moore Lappé and Schurman go a step further and argue that even poverty need not pose an obstacle, so long as human rights are distributed.

Pointing to relatively poor countries like China, Sri Lanka and Burma, which achieved a fall in fertility, they concluded that the 'political, economic, and cultural changes that allowed population growth to slow dramatically did not depend upon first achieving high per capita income' (1989, p. 68).

The view that redistribution can take place and patterns of fertility growth can change regardless of socio-economic circumstances is open to question. Redistribution in the context of poverty can have only a declaratory character. The fact that people are equally poor, rather than just poor, need not have a decisive influence on the culture of fertility. Nor is it clear why some societies like Burma or China should be characterized as any more enlightened than many others in Asia. It is not at all self-evident how the fall in fertility in these countries is linked to enlightened social policy. The link between progressive social policies and population stabilization is also far from apparent in the case of South Korea and Taiwan, where the fall in the growth of population was even greater than, say, in the case of China. The association of equity with the lowering of the rate of fertility is far from straightforward.

Upon closer examination, it becomes evident that redistribution is often a euphemism for policies designed to influence fertility. That is why most redistributionist arguments invariably culminate with a call for changing the position of women in developing societies. This conclusion is based on the belief that any improvement in the position of women would lead to a reduction in population growth. The goal of influencing fertility behaviour through women is central to the redistributionist emphasis. As the authors of *Beyond the Limits* (1992) argue:

> The factors believed to be most directly important in lowering birth rates are not so much the average national level of income, but the extent to which that income actually changes the lives of families, and especially the lives of women. More important than GNP per capita are factors such as education and employment (especially for women), family planning, and reduction of infant mortality (Meadows, Meadows and Randers, 1992, p. 29).

For these authors, the key problem is overpopulation. Redistribution and especially the change in the position of women are seen as a means of influencing fertility. Not surprisingly, whenever a list of redistributive measures is drawn up, it always just happens to include family planning. In this way population control is repackaged as a welfare measure. The need to find new ways of justifying population control must be part of the explanation as to why, in the early eighties, the population lobby adopted the rhetoric of equity and of women's rights.

Those who advocate the perspective of redistribution are often motivated by a zeal to improve the position of poor people and of women. The language that is used to promote this perspective tends to be sympathetic to the plight of people in developing societies. Yet despite its stated intentions, the redistributionist perspective can inadvertently reinforce cultural domination. Many values promoted to encourage family nucleation – such as gender equality, individual rights – are in and of themselves unobjectionable. But is it acceptable to place outside pressure on other societies to accept such values? Riedmann has observed that one consequence of this intrusion is the introduction of the Western value of relativism. In surveys on attitudes to family size, respondents were assured that 'there is no right or wrong answer' (1993, p. 67). But by posing questions from the standpoint of Western relativism the investigators were implicitly questioning the world view of their respondents. The very acceptance of the view that there could be a diversity of reproductive practices would undermine the Yoruba tradition. Moreover, the questioning of the legitimacy of prevailing Yoruba reproductive practices questions an entire way of life.

In the past, modernization theory offered liberal democracy and individualistic behaviour as the solution to underdevelopment. Through experience, this form of social engineering has been discredited. Now modernization theory is recycled in the form of advocating social and gender equality as a way of stabilizing the growth of population. Even with the very best of intentions, is there not a danger that the targeting of certain traditional practices will become a destructive engagement acting against a people's chosen way of life?

7

Targeting Women

Since the late eighties the central theme of population policy has become the empowerment of women. An assessment of the Cairo Conference on Population noted in passing, that during the proceedings 'no plenary speaker dared omit at least mentioning' the importance of empowerment of women. It added that 'agreement on the central role of women in development has become so non-controversial that it was not even an issue at the IPCD'.[1] An examination of most of the recent publications on the subject shows that the role of women has become a dominant theme in the literature on demography. And yet this consensus around the position of women is a relatively recent development. It can be seen as an integral part of the reorientation towards redistribution and more specifically towards influencing the culture of fertility in Third World societies.

7.1 The Discovery of Women

Because of women's central role in reproduction, their attitude and behaviour has been of interest to those involved in population issues from the beginning of the eugenic tradition to today. Pronatalists have demanded that women carry out their duty and breed more children for the nation, while anti-natalists counselled the opposite point of view. For example the American President,

Theodore Roosevelt, advised married middle-class white women to bear at least four children, to ensure that their race did not lose out to more prolific competitors.[2] A discussion on this subject in 1907, published in *The American Journal of Sociology*, focused on the attitude of women to child-bearing. Edward Ross argued that emancipated women regarded pregnancy from the perspective of 'heavy physiological and personal cost' and therefore opted for smaller families. Women, freed from many of their traditional obligations, were not restricted to their role as mothers, and were often able to consider pursuing a career outside family life. This individualization of women, according to Ross, was another important factor which influenced fertility. 'The struggle of woman to realise an individuality has obliged her to rebel against her Biblical status and to spurn the counsel of submission to the curse of Eve; so that the progress of unbelief is not without bearing on the decline of the birth-rate', wrote Ross. Ross supported these secular developments. But he feared that while middle-class white people practised restraint, they would lose their power to rule other races which continued to multiply.[3] In subsequent discussions on demographic change, the link between the amelioration in the social position of women and the decline in family size was clearly established.

Curiously, despite an appreciation of the way in which progress towards women's emancipation could impact upon fertility, the population lobby did not take this connection seriously until the late sixties. It was the rise of the women's liberation movement which alerted the population establishment to its potential importance. The women's liberation movement was dynamic and possessed considerable moral authority. At a time when the population lobby lacked any popular legitimacy, the temptation to link up with the women's movement must have been strong. Those interested in population control saw the demand of the women's movement for access to contraception and abortion as lending credibility to their own agenda. The potential importance of the women's movement for the population lobby was spelled out in 1972, by the American political scientist Peter Bachrach: 'The interest of supporters of population control would be significantly served if they used their power to aid women's liberation groups to realise one of their goals – compelling the government to enforce its policy of providing for equal education and economic opportunities for women – for the anti-natalist sentiment that would be generated by such an enforcement would be profound'.[4]

The proposition, that the advance of the women's movement would help to create a climate in which anti-natalist ideas could enjoy legitimacy, won significant support in the population field.

By the early seventies, many of the high profile population controllers had jumped on the women's bandwagon. Increasingly they came to regard the export of women's issues to the Third World as an important component of indirect population programmes. The Ehrlichs were particularly enthusiastic about promoting population policies through the medium of women's rights. They outlined their approach:

> There are many possibilities in the sphere of family structure, sexual mores, and the status of women that can be explored . . . With some exceptions, women have traditionally been allowed to fulfil only the roles of wife and mother. Anything that can be done to diminish the emphasis upon these roles and provide women with equal opportunities in education, employment and other areas is likely to reduce the birth rate. Any measures that postpone marriage, especially for women, would also help to encourage the reduction in birth rates (1970, p. 253).

Here was a bold platform designed to harness the dynamism of the women's liberation movement to the cause of population control. From this perspective, changes in the position of women could provide the answer that the population lobby had for long been looking for in its search for a good argument.

Since the seventies, the issue of women's position in society has provided the population lobby with a considerable degree of legitimacy to pursue its objective. Even those normally hostile to egalitarian causes have integrated women's issues into their arguments. So, Garrett Hardin, whose book sought to mobilize anti-immigration sentiment to boost population control, also adopts the instrumentalist approach to the issue of women that is characteristic of the contemporary literature. 'A most optimistic harbinger of the future is the women's liberation movement. The world over, there is no question but that the greatest progress in reducing birth rates is occurring in societies in which women have been most liberated from male domination' (1993, p. 308). The connection between the changing status of women and the reduction in family size has been enthusiastically embraced by most sections of the population lobby as an important theme in their campaign. The targeting of women is now routine in the various surveys and reports on population. The report of the International Commission on Peace and Food (1994) clearly expressed this sentiment: 'concrete steps must be taken to generate greater educational, training and employment opportunities for the poor, and most especially for females – the best-known methods for eradicating poverty and bringing down the rate of population growth' (p. 186). Since changing the position of women is apparently the 'best known' method for bringing down the rate of population, it has been adopted as a policy by all the relevant agencies.

The issue of women's status is only the most recent of a long line of causes adopted – development, poverty, environment, equity – to justify population policies. From this standpoint, the subjugation of women is important because of its effect on the rate of fertility, rather than a problem in its own terms. So one survey of global demographic trends is critical of 'bias against women' since it 'may also be the most important cause of rapid population growth' (Far East Economic Review, 1994, p. 70). For Stanley Johnson, director of the European Commission, the emancipation of women is the key for solving the population problem, since 'a lasting fall in fertility will only be achieved through greater female emancipation.'[5]

Many women writers and feminists have been disturbed by the way their concerns have been manipulated and co-opted by the population activists. Bonnie Mass was one of the first women to warn against this manipulation of feminist rhetoric, arguing that imperialism had veiled 'its interest behind the mask of false feminism'. She pointed to how female oriented propaganda had become a device for selling population control (Mass, 1976, pp. 230–1). Amrit Wilson has warned against the 'cynical attempt' to use feminist rhetoric against women, and Lakshmi Lingam commented that the incorporation of women's reproductive rights into the population agenda in practice meant that 'the rhetoric of the feminist movement' was being appropriated, though not its concerns. She wrote: 'At present women's status or health is being seen as a means to an end in the following way: improving women's status speeds fertility decline thus reducing considerably "the overall negative impact" of population on environment and development'.[6] Third World women's groups have also expressed suspicion about the manner in which reproductive rights have been co-opted into the international population agenda.

Many feminist writers are not so much hostile as ambivalent in their relationship to the population lobby. The contribution of Betsy Hartmann well illustrates this tendency. Her book *Reproductive Rights and Wrongs* (1987) provided a well-documented critique

of the ideology and practices of the population lobby. Moreover
Hartmann was sensitive to the instrumental way in which the issue
of women was used by international agencies. She warned that
feminists were in danger of being outflanked, noting that 'there is
always the danger that these individuals' genuine commitment to
women's welfare will be twisted and manipulated by others in the
population establishment who want to appropriate feminist language and concepts in order to give population control a better
image' (p. 295). Despite these reservations, Hartmann did not
reject population policies as such. She was prepared to give some
initiatives the benefit of a doubt and called for an alliance with
'liberal family planners' against what she called the 'hardline
population camp' (p. 143).

Hartmann's call for an alliance of feminists and liberal family
planners reflects a clear tendency within the international population establishment. Most feminists argue that redistribution, equity and improvement in the position of women should be the key
element in any population policy. Many of them are aware of the
instrumental way in which these issues are used. However, because they accept a common premise, that population growth is the
problem, their criticism of the more traditional population lobby
tends to have only a tactical character.

The Development Alternatives with Women for a New
Era (DAWN) clearly reflects the ambivalent relationship between
feminists and the population lobby. Sonia Correa, writing from a
DAWN perspective, is aware of the danger of 'potential manipulation' of its concerns by the population establishment. Nevertheless, she argued that 'despite the risks of manipulation, in DAWN's
view women must apply pressure and negotiate with the development establishment (including the population community) to carve
out our own political space' (1994, p. 64). Correa is convinced that
there is a two-way relationship between feminists and the population lobby. She contends that organizations like DAWN have
succeeded in influencing the population community. 'As a result
of many years of women's determined organising and lobbying
internationally, the population field will never again be the same'
(p. 67). In one sense Correa's observation is a reasonable one. The
influence of the issue of women on the population lobby is considerable. However, seen from a different perspective, it could be
argued that the adoption of feminist concerns was a small price to
pay in exchange for involving sections of the women's movement
in the population field.

Though there is a pragmatic acceptance of the issue of women by most population activists, the tension between the organizations like DAWN and the traditional population lobby are far from resolved. In one case the priority is to improve the position of women, in the other it is to reduce the growth of population. These different points of view can coexist because both sides accept the premise that in some sense the growth of population is a problem. For example, Gita Sen and Caren Grown take issue with traditional population policies, for what they consider is their lack of sensitivity to the needs of women. However, such objections accept the fundamentals of population concern and thereby endow it with credibility. Their criticism is situated within the confines of a demographic agenda which locates population growth as the *a priori* problem. So when they criticize 'programmes that do not take the interest of women into account' on the grounds that they are 'unlikely to succeed', they appeal to the commonly accepted criterion of effectiveness (1988, p. 48). Implicitly, such arguments raise questions about whether the criterion of effectiveness is consistent with the promotion of women's welfare.

In practice, the tension between the priority of population control and of improvement in the position of women remains unresolved. This is not merely due to a conflict of priorities. Whereas the precondition for the emancipation of women is far-reaching socio-economic change, population policies merely require organization and effective targeting. Consequently, the commitment to change the position of women is treated as a long-term objective, while family programmes are seen as practicable in the here and now. For example critics of India's Draft National Population Policy have pointed to the cynical way in which in practice the role of women is ignored: 'the report is virtually silent on the growing feminisation of poverty in India. Its reference to gender equity and to free and informed choice for women merely reflect the report's uncritical and deliberate assimilation of the vocabulary of women's groups and women activists'.[7]

One reason why the tension between the two priorities remains unresolved is that at the level of policy-making, anti-poverty measures have gone out of fashion. Since the eighties, international agencies have promoted structural adjustment programmes, whose effect has been the intensification of inequalities in developing societies. Many of the international agencies who have called for a greater integration of women into population policies have also promoted structural adjustment programmes. It is surprising that

the contradiction between these two objectives has not been rigor-
ously explored by the protagonists in the debate.[8]

Feminist criticisms of traditional population policy often focus
on the techniques used and the manner of their administration.
Some of this literature has usefully drawn attention to coercive
practices deployed in the management of family planning programmes. One of the dominant issues explored in this literature is
the problems associated with contraceptive technology. Indeed in
many cases, the object of concern is with different contraceptive
techniques, rather than with the premise of population control.
Such technical criticisms rarely challenge the fundamental perspective of the population lobby. They often fail to tackle the social
dynamic behind population policy.

There also exists a feminist perspective which is irreconcilably
opposed to population policies. A network of women's groups
opposed to population policies issued a Declaration in December
1993, which argued that there 'cannot be any feminist population
policy because it violates and contradicts the basic premise of
feminism'. The Declaration accused the population establishment
of hiding its motives by 'cloaking them in words hijacked from the
women's liberation movement' and seeks to reclaim the language
of feminism for women.[9] Farida Akter, from Bangladesh has
written extensively on this subject. She decried The World Bank's
targeting of women: 'The World Bank doesn't have any development perspective on women, it just sees them as a mean of reducing
fertility rates. That is why they educate girls; that is why mothers'
clubs and co-operatives are encouraged. It even insists that girls
have to drop out of the scholarship programme if they get married.'[10] Akter's uncompromising opposition to population policy
has made her a target of considerable invective from her opponents.

It is not just the population lobby which has sought to use the
issue of women to realize its objectives. Pro-natalist critics of
population policies often adopt a feminist vocabulary to justify
their case. In particular they have sought to publicize cases where
women have been coerced to accept birth control programmes.
They have also sought to build upon the widespread hostility that
exists in feminist circles towards specific forms of contraceptive
technology. They have publicized women's programmes that are
actually no more then population programmes. Examples, such as
that of the Bangladeshi experience, have provided pro-natalist
publicists with ammunition.

Western anti-abortion organizations have sought to use feminist criticisms of population policies for their own ends. Many of their publications are expressly distanced from the abortion issue and stress feminist concern with contraceptive technology. In this way, their less popular argument against a woman's right to choose is submerged in a mass of detail about the wrongs of population control. For example, the *Population Information Pack* (1994), published by the Committee on Population and the Economy is expressly designed to mobilize feminist hostility to the population establishment. Such groups seek to build on feminist criticism of reproductive technology, and link these anxieties to their own cause. Their instrumental use of the issue of women mirrors that of their ideological opponents.

Some Malthusian feminists are sensitive to the possibility that the anti-abortionist forces might exploit the hostile reaction to population policies. Ruth Dixon-Mueller has conceded that past 'efforts at population control have triggered resistance from many quarters based on charges of cultural insensitivity, program abuses, and even genocide' (1993, p. xii). Dixon-Mueller's main concern was to avoid the 'potentially devastating co-optation of feminist criticism by anti-feminist, "right-to-life" organisations' (p.33). Clearly all sides in the population debate will continue to seek alliances with feminists in order to boost their campaign.

7.2 Educating Women

Policies which are formally oriented towards women do not automatically alter their social position. This is not surprising, since any serious improvement in the status of women would require a major change in the way that society is organized. Today's policies tend to have the more modest goal of changing women's attitudes through education, rather than altering their status in society. This approach is driven by the widely held assumption that the education of women is one of the most effective ways of regulating the rate of fertility. It is generally believed that education is a powerful influence on the rate of fertility, since it changes the way that women regard themselves. It is suggested that education offers women more choices and greater independence. Many policy-makers contend that female education is a good investment, since it directly contributes to reducing the rate of fertility. That is why

the Indian demographer, Ashish Bose, argued that 'the expenditure on female literacy should be the first charge on the
family planning budget'. Writing in the same vein, the Nor-
wegian economist Stein Hansen calculates that 'investment in
girls' education also yields global development returns in the
form of reduced population pressure via delayed age of
marriage.' According to Hansen, the consequence of such delayed age of marriage 'would be 1 billion fewer of us before
global population is reached'.[11] Experts argue that women's education is good value for money – some suggest that in terms of
its impact on fertility it is even more effective then economic
redistribution.

There is considerable evidence of a correlation between education and the rate of fertility. Many studies point out that women
with education, particularly a high level of education, marry at a
later age, know more about contraception and have fewer children
then those without such schooling. For example, in Peru, women
with advanced levels of education have on average 2.7 children,
whereas those without such qualifications average 6.2 children. In
Uganda and Liberia, women with higher education are reported to
have on average five births in comparison to seven births for
women with primary education.[12] It is not surprising that Moore
Lappé and Schurman have concluded that in 'one study after
another, women's education turns out to be the single most consistent predictor of lower fertility' (1989, p. 25).

However, the relationship between the education of women and
levels of fertility is not at all straightforward. It is not legitimate to
isolate education as an independent variable that evolves of its
own accord. Education does not take place in a social vacuum. It is
often part of a wider nexus of change which involves urbanization,
social dislocation and individuation. For example, urbanized
women have greater access to both education and contraceptive
services than those living in rural communities. In such circumstances the relationship between the education of women and the
rate of fertility is not simply one of cause and effect. Most recent
studies suggest that the impact of education on women's fertility
is 'contingent on the level of economic development, on social
structure, and on cultural milieu'.[13]

Numerous studies have indicated that the relationship between
female education and the rate of fertility is far from self-evident.
Caldwell has pointed to the 'weak associations between fertility
decline and education in Kenya'. Carol Vlassoff's study of wom-

en's status and fertility in a Maharashtra village indicated that perhaps the influence of marriage distance was more significant then education. Vlassoff concluded that the complex ways in which education regulates fertility 'remain a mystery'.[14] Others point to urbanization as an important variable – educated women are not merely educated, they are also urbanized. And in an urban situation the economic contribution of children to the family is far less than in a rural context, which means less pressure to have large families (Brydon and Chant, 1989, pp. 199–200). In her discussion of the link between education and fertility, Julia Mosse is right to insist that in this discussion 'a correlation is not the same as a causal relationship.'[15]

The preoccupation with women's education and status is motivated by the belief that this is the area where intervention can be most effective in helping to reduce fertility. According to Hartmann, population research is directed towards isolating those variables which will be most effective in curbing fertility. She describes this perspective of attempting to influence fertility directly through policies like the provision of education as 'the isolation exercise'. Hartmann argues that such a one-dimensional policy is unlikely to achieve positive results since change is a holistic process. Pointing to societies like Cuba, Korea and Sri Lanka, which have passed through the demographic transition, she noted that the goal was not 'a reduction in the birth rate, but *development in its own right*, of which fertility control was simply one of many aspects and not the most important in terms of improving the quality of people's lives' (1987, pp. 284–5).

A sociological conception of change raises questions about the exact nature of the relationship between the position of women and fertility decline. Many of the models used to illustrate the impact of women's education on fertility decline isolate this relationship from the broader social patterns at work. Invariably, the relevance of such models is open to more than one interpretation. Let's take the example of the Indian state of Kerala. Proponents of women oriented population policy most frequently cite Kerala as a model of how income redistribution, mass education and improvement in the position of women has led to a fall in the rate of birth. Many authors seem convinced that a mix of progressive policies accounts for the decline of family size in Kerala. For example, Hartmann has argued that mass participation and an egalitarian ethos is responsible for Kerala's positive achievements (1987, pp. 281–3). Amartya Sen praised Kerala for 'encouraging and creating conditions for reasoned decisions and enlightened rational behaviour'.[16]

And yet it is possible to argue that there are other, wider forces at work, which provide insights into Kerala's fertility decline. Although poor, the state of Kerala has undergone major social change, over a long period of time. It is difficult to sustain the thesis that recent Government policies were responsible for the relatively high rate of female literacy, since Kerala has an impressive record in this sphere that goes back to the nineteenth century. According to one account, the 'picture that emerges of the Kerala women at the beginning of the twentieth century is that there were ample opportunities available to them to get free education at all levels'. Clearly, female education has evolved organically over a long period and has little to do with any one-off progressive policy. In fact, this tradition of female education must be understood in relation to the wider position of women in society. The matrilineal institution of inheritance through the female line suggests that women have possessed influence in Kerala society for some time.[17]

The position of women in Kerala is directly linked to the peculiar experience of social change in the region. One outcome of its historical development has been its unusually cosmopolitan social structure. Aside from the majority Hindu community, it has the highest Christian population of all the states in the Indian sub-continent. It also has a substantial Muslim population. The tendency towards a relatively cosmopolitan culture was reinforced by the relatively weak role of traditional rural communities. According to Nayar, one of the unique features of Kerala's economy has been the absence of the village system that is typical in most of India. This gave each family household a greater scope in decision-making, which in turn encouraged the growth of individualism. Nayar remarked that, 'it was inevitable that the spirit of individualism should pervade not only the male sex but the female sex as well.'[18]

The growth of individualism was confirmed by the speed with which Kerala has made the transition from joint families to nuclear families. Often the legacy of individuation is the erosion of custom and tradition. New life-styles emerge and relations between the sexes are altered. Sociologists from Durkheim onwards have pointed to factors like the incidence of suicide as a symptom of the process of social atomization. The state of Kerala, which has the highest rate of suicide in India, certainly fits this Durkheimian model.[19] Given these important changes, especially the shift towards the establishment of nuclear families, the relatively low rate of fertility of Kerala is not that surprising. It is these changes, rather than a specific policy, which may explain Kerala's demographic pattern. In passing it is worth noting that the record of women's advance in Kerala is not straightforward either. For example, nearly ninety per cent of marriages in Kerala are still 'arranged' marriages.

An interesting counter-example to the Kerala experience is the Indian state of Tamil Nadu. The total fertility rate of India in 1989 was 3.9. For Tamil Nadu (2.5) it was almost as low as that of Kerala (2.0). Tamil Nadu and Kerala are the only Indian states with a total fertility rate below 3.0, and yet Tamil Nadu exhibits none of the redistributionist virtues which are meant to be responsible for low rates of fertility. As Savitri wrote: 'Tamil Nadu seems to be a counter-example to many of the widely accepted hypotheses that lower infant mortality rate, higher literacy and better status of women are a must for bringing down fertility'. So why did people in Tamil Nadu opt for smaller families? Although the answer is far from conclusive, Savitri provides an important clue, observing that Tamil Nadu has the 'highest composite index of urbanisation in India'.[20] The main influence on the fall in fertility in Tamil Nadu is likely to be the impact of urbanization. The urban milieu influences rural communities. Rural–urban linkages are strong so that even people living in the rural areas can find employment in the urban setting, without shifting their place of residence. It may well be that it is this common experience of urbanization which explains why these two states have achieved such marked reductions in the rate of fertility.

At the very least, arguments which attempt to forge a causal relationship between the changing status of women and fertility decline are in danger of ignoring the effect of wider structural change. It may also be that the relationship is not one of cause and effect. There are certainly many examples of patriarchal societies in Europe which have experienced demographic transition without improving the position of women. Other examples are Japan and the countries of South East Asia. Geoffrey McNicoll of the Population Council has questioned the widely held view that only 'if gender biases are rooted out' will 'women be able to escape poverty and choose to have fewer children'. McNicoll wrote:

> To take only the most obvious counter-example, the massive fertility decline in east Asia starting in the 1960s (and much earlier in Japan) has occurred in societies still notably patriarchal – some, indeed, displaying

the most blatant male chauvinism. .... The cross-sectional data on fertility by mother's education that is trundled out to support the policy line, giving full weight to what is often a tiny fraction of women with post-secondary schooling, is more likely to be capturing an incompletely controlled effect of social class than a differential that will respond to measures that lift female enrolment'.[21]

McNicoll is right to question simplistic assumptions about the magical effects of education on the rate of fertility. It is also evident that education does not exist in isolation from other crucial social experiences. The effect of education cannot be measured without considering the impact of urbanization, social mobility and economic development.

Ultimately, the central role which the population lobby now assigns to educating women is driven by pragmatism. Unlike the far-reaching measures demanded by development or even a package of income redistribution, education appears to offer a cheaper and more direct way of influencing fertility. Moreover, the association of such population programmes with redistribution and women's equality helps to give them broader legitimacy.

7.3 Propaganda for Influencing Fertility

The interweaving of population and women's policy is confusing. This confusion is perpetuated by the tendency of contributors to the discussion to accept the presentation of family planning policies at face value. One of the questions regarding family planning programmes that is rarely posed is this: are they about improving the position of women or are they about controlling population? In their discussion of such policies, writers rarely distinguish between the public relations packaging, the fundamental aims, and the means used to implement them. Consequently, even those critical of population policies seldom entertain the conclusion that they might have little to do with the stated goal of improving the position of women.

In most case studies of population programmes, policies oriented towards women's status and education are presented as motivated by demographic considerations. Critics who demand that such policies be less instrumentalist towards women miss the point of why such programmes exist, and why international agencies finance them in the first place. If for example, the real objective

was the improvement of female education then it would be promoted independently of demographic considerations. But that
would presuppose that education was the end rather than the
means to realize another agenda. The insistence that family planning programmes increase their emphasis on women misses this
point. Even when such programmes talk about nothing else but
women, the issue of equality remains an expedient to be manipulated for demographic objectives. An illustration of this is Lily
Hsia's editorial in a recent issue of the *Journal of Nurse-Midwifery*,
entitled 'Stemming the tide of the global population explosion: The
key role of women'. Hsia celebrates the increasing importance
attached to the role of women by family planners. However an
examination of her argument reveals that the position of women is
peripheral to the discussion: 'In the past, family planning was
considered to be the most effective means to stabilise and slow
world population growth. Today, other initiatives such as quality
reproductive health care, increased educational and economic
opportunities for women, reduction in infant and child mortality
rates, and increased employment of women are considered important adjuncts to population decline'.[22] It is in the capacity of
'adjuncts to population decline' that women's issues acquire relevance in demographic discourse. In the same vein, an article
'Empowering women: An essential objective', published in the *UN
Chronicle*, goes straight to the point. Its opening sentence, reads;
'the empowerment of women – a basic human rights objective – is
key to achieving development and population goals.'[23]

The emphasis of demography on women is heavily influenced
by the objective of winning the propagandist war against the critics
of population policy. That demographic narrative is shaped by the
exigencies of public relations and propaganda has already been
alluded to. The need publicly to distance population policy from
traditional Western anti-natalist objectives became increasingly
important in the seventies. During that period, demography self-
consciously divested itself of the remnants of its past eugenic and
racist vocabulary. Traditional welfare issues, health and the status
of women were used to repackage population policies. An important component of this shift in vocabulary was the adoption of a
more indirect approach to population control. The implications of
this approach were clearly spelled out in an important American
Government document titled 'Implications of worldwide population growth for US security and overseas interests'.[24]

The document argued that population policies designed for the

Third World, had to be presented as if they were motivated by altruism rather than national self-interest. To 'minimise charges of an imperialist motivation behind its support of population activities', it was suggested that programmes had to be presented as if they were about social reform. The document also suggested that terms like 'population control' and 'birth control' should be avoided by personnel implementing such programmes in the Third World. Like other reports, this one proposed that population programmes should be disguised as a service promoting health or some other public good. It noted:

> In the case of LDC countries uncommitted to population programs our efforts must be fine-tuned to their particular sensitivities and attitudes. In the main, we should avoid the language of 'birth control' in favour of 'family planning' or 'responsible parenthood', with the emphasis being placed on child spacing in the interests of the health of child and mother and the well-being of the family and community. Introduction and extension of primary health services are, in fact, the principal ways of successfully introducing family planning into many of these countries.

The introduction of population control through the back door – under cover of concern about health, education, etc. – was a central component of the strategy. A final component of this approach was the use of intermediaries for promoting population policies. The document advocated the use of non-governmental organizations and other agencies not directly linked with Washington as the appropriate vehicles for implementing population policies.

The propaganda techniques used by the population lobby today rely on the use of intermediary organizations. Such organizations – groups of women, health professionals, community groups – are sometimes set up with the explicit aim of creating a demand for population policies. According to Howard Wiarda 'considerable pains have been taken to disguise' US Government involvement in population programmes. He noted;

> Much of the funding has been channelled through third-party agencies to disguise the extent of United States involvement. Various fronts have been set up to make it appear, particularly in the early stages as though it is a private association that is supporting the program, not the United States government . . . Care has also been taken to find local doctors and concerned citizens in the countries affected so as to provide the appearance of local control, even though the funding and much of the direction may come from outside'.[25]

It is worth noting that the US Government does not have a

monopoly on the use of front organizations. Such front organizations, claiming to represent authentic local interests, are routinely deployed by both sides of the population debate.

The promotion of population policies through the rhetoric of health, particularly women's health is one of the most important innovations of the propaganda techniques that emerged in the seventies. Programmes that were once labelled as policies of 'population control' and then called 'birth control' only to change to 'family planning', now go under the appellation of 'reproductive health'. The integration of population programmes into health services has become central to the marketing of fertility control. This medicalization of population concern is seldom contested, because it appears to be entirely about the non-controversial subject of health.

The medicalization of population control has been central to the approach adopted by Western governments since the late seventies. For example, a report commissioned by the American Government in 1981 advised that population activities 'should be integrated with maternal and health care delivery' because projects that focus too narrowly on family planning as a solution 'only increase suspicion in the host country'.[26] Since the early eighties, it has become customary unobtrusively to insert population measures into a broader health initiative. In that way, fertility control is presented as part of a long list of health measures. Invariably population control is promoted as a major contribution to women's health. With this redefinition of the objective of family planning, patients may be excused for failing to grasp that contraception is about reducing numbers of children.

In response to the demands of public relations, the term reproductive health has been expanded to include virtually every women's condition, from menstruation to menopause. In this way, the underlying agenda of fertility control becomes inconspicuous to the designated target audience. Ironically, some radical critics advocate the expansion of the meaning of reproductive health, since they believe that it represents an important step in the direction of a more holistic women oriented approach. Gita Sen argues that there has been important progress because 'women's health activists have increasingly joined the population debate' (Sen, Germain and Chen, 1994, p. 63). This optimistic interpretation can be countered by the view that women's health has become the latest in a long line of fashionable policies through which the population lobby seeks to influence fertility.

Reproductive health, like education has become in practice another form of isolation exercise, aimed at reducing fertility. Reproductive health is above all about the indirect administration of contraception. Like education, the issue of health in general is isolated from wider issues of social development for the specific objective of influencing fertility. From the perspective of human well-being, the isolation of health is necessarily counterproductive since it is so much bound up with every aspect of social life. This point is well made by Rosa Linda Valenzona in her criticism of the manipulation of the health issue by the 1993 Philippine Demographic Survey:

> The document concludes that the high risk infant, neonatal, child and maternal mortality is associated with pregnancies where mothers are too young, too old, or have already had several children. But a discussion of poverty is missing from the list of factors related to health. It would be difficult to deny that poverty, lack of access to safe water, poor housing, poor hygiene and unsanitary conditions all have a strong bearing on the health of the mother and child.[27]

Health programmes which fail to tackle the issue of poverty are either just ineffective or are promoting an agenda which has little to do with human well-being.

Many health activists would concur with Valenzona's criticism of the neglect of the crucial role of poverty. But in some cases the narrow emphasis on health, and specifically on birth control is interpreted as just an isolated error. Ines Smyth's discussion of the Safe Motherhood campaign in Indonesia accepts that it gives 'too much importance to family planning as a strategy to reduce maternal mortality'. But she adds that there is 'insufficient evidence to suggest that there is a sinister explanation for the stress that Safe Motherhood initiatives give to family planning'. So how does she account for the emphasis of the campaign? 'However, it is common to consider reproductive health primarily from a demographic perspective and to link it to family planning. The cost-saving benefits of family planning over the more radical measures necessary to improve women's general and reproductive health are perhaps a more realistic explanation of this emphasis'.[28] Smyth is loath to draw out the implications of her own words. If health is promoted from a 'demographic perspective' then the central objective is not the well-being of women but the reduction of population. Campaigns that are genuinely committed to reduce the rate of maternal mortality would be driven by a concern with maternal mortality and not something else. This is not what motivates the Safe Motherhood campaign. The Safe Motherhood campaign uses the issue of maternal mortality to influence the fertility of Indonesian women. It is the failure of many health activists to demand the separation of health from what Smyth calls a demographic perspective that has allowed population programmes to masquerade as projects about reproductive rights.

The failure to demand the separation of health from demography or of education from demography or of poverty from demography is not accidental. Even the most critical voices are often trapped by their own consciousness of demography. Left-wing writers, feminists and health activists often accept the premise of the population lobby. Sometimes, their criticism of narrow population policy is grounded in a shared perception of the fundamentals. The arguments of Sen, Germain and Chen for a radical and empowering policy is instructive in this respect. 'We argue that investing in people's health, empowerment, and human rights is not only worthy in its own right, but would probably be more conducive to population stabilisation than narrowly conceived policies of population control' (1994, p.11). To justify investment in health in terms of its contribution to the stabilization of population is to elide the distinction between two very different concerns. Such arguments offer only a minimalist alternative to traditional population policies. To the 'narrowly conceived policies of population control' they counterpose a more widely conceived programme. A difference in scale but not of substance!

The objective of this chapter has not been to question the motives of individuals involved in the various programmes discussed above. It is concerned with the consequences, sometimes the unintended consequences of an acceptance of a demographic perspective on redistribution and women. The contention here is that, in most programmes to do with poverty, education, health, or the position of women, the imperative of influencing fertility tends to prevail. Typically, such programmes turn into an exercise in isolation. The discussion begins with broad questions like redistribution, poverty or the status of women. It then moves onto the more narrow terrain of education and health. And on this ground the only durable theme is the provision of contraception. Somehow every project manages to introduce contraception into its activities. For example, an agricultural credit union in Bangladesh which lends to poor rural women was persuaded by international donors to make borrowers agree to abide by a strict code of conduct, including 'good family planning methods' before loans were approved (OECD, 1988, p. 62). This association of a demographic perspective with a financial transaction is no more absurd than, say, its link with education. It merely shows that these days population policies come in the most unexpected packages.

8

Enivronmentalism to the Rescue

Of all the innovations in the discussion of demography, the most effective to date has been the attempt to link the so-called population problem to concerns about the environment. This synthesis of environmental with population concern has had a major impact on the popular imagination. Unlike conventional Malthusian dangers, which only affect those directly concerned, the environment-population synthesis is evocatively represented as a threat to everyone. As Christa Wichterich pointed out: 'where people in the Third World allegedly bring about their own hunger by their increase, they only injure themselves: but where they allegedly use up the resources that we want to consume, and disturb the ecological balance, which is necessary for the survival of all humanity, they are also injuring us'.[1] According to this schema, population pressure in one part of the world, leading to environmental degradation, poses a danger to the rest of the globe. In this way the population problem becomes truly globalized. What Wichterich has described as the 'apocalyptic trinity of population growth, scarcity of resources and destruction of the environment' provides this ecological version of the Malthusian model with considerable force. A simplistic but highly influential formula states that population growth contributes to the destruction of the environment, thereby endangering all forms of life. The influence of such sensationalist sentiments can be found in many of the international reports dealing with global problems published over the past decade.

Our Global Neighbourhood, the report of the Commission on Global Governance, provides a representative account of the environment–population synthesis. The report presented a vision of a world endangered by too many human beings:

> Rapid growth in population is closely linked to the issue of environmental security through the impact that people have on the earth's life-supporting resources. Evidence has accumulated of widespread ecological degradation resulting from human activity: soils losing fertility or being eroded, overgrazed grasslands, desertification, dwindling fisheries, disappearing species, shrinking forests, polluted air and water. These have been joined by the newer problems of climate change and ozone depletion. Together they threaten to make the earth less habitable and life more hazardous' (1995, p. 29).

The underlying logic at work in this analysis isolates population growth as the cause of every form of the environmental crisis. 'It is realistic, then, to offer the generalized conclusion that *population growth plays a prominent and probably predominant part in environmental problems*', as one well known proponent of this argument put it.[2] In some versions, this argument has acquired the character of a veritable panic. Readers are left in little doubt that 'the future of the planet hangs in the balance'.

Although fears about the environment were sometimes linked to population growth in the past, only in recent times has it become the dominant theme in demographic discourse. Wilmoth and Ball's interesting review of the history of the population debate in American popular magazines shows that this theme gained ascendancy only in the eighties. The authors noted a dramatic shift from arguments which focused on underdevelopment to those concentrating on the environment.[3]

One explanation for the remarkable shift of demographic concerns towards the environment motif is that it helped mobilize new sources of funding. This is the explanation that Sonia Correa offered as to why the 'rationale for population control in the 1990s has moved away from a traditional economic development argument to a case for environmental balance' (1994, p. 13). Finance aside, the promotion of the environment–population synthesis has allowed the population lobby to plug into a movement that commands authority and respect. It was the 'environmentalist fever' which swept the United States that helped launch the official Population Commission in 1970. By recasting traditional population fears in an environmental form, the arguments acquired greater public impact.

In the sixties, when the environmental concerns began to surface, only a few individuals blamed population growth. Paul Ehrlich was the most high profile advocate of this line of thought. He pioneered the approach which presented environmental degradation as the consequence of too many people. 'Too many cars, too many factories, too much pesticide . . . too little water, too much carbon dioxide – all can be traced easily to *too many people*', concluded Ehrlich (1971, p. 36). While many of the arguments against population growth – such as the exigencies of development – have been abandoned, those associated with the environment have gained strength. Many advocates of population policy acknowledge that arguments about the environment, unlike those about economic development, have proved to be effective. This environmental orientation has helped rescue the Malthusian case. Geoffrey McNicoll of the Population Council is clear on this point: 'The downgrading by some economists of the seriousness of rapid population growth . . . qualified as a shock – calling into question what had been the principal rationale for population programs. In the event, this foundational damage was less severe than it first seemed and was largely offset in its effect by an upgrading of worry about population growth by environmentalists.'[4] The issue of the environment, like that of the status of women discussed in the previous chapter, has helped give contemporary coherence to the anti-natalist perspective.

The fusion of population and environmental concerns is often forced. Invariably the historical causes of environmental problems in the Third World – for example the impact of colonialism – are glossed over. There is also little consideration of the way in which the integration of agricultural societies into the world market contributed to the degradation of land – for example through monocultural practices. Instead, population is isolated as an independent variable that is principally responsible for environmental destruction.

The traditional Malthusian warnings about diminishing food supplies are now rarely raised by serious writers. The Malthusian literature is far less specific about the object of its fears than in the past. Many authors concede that the world's population can be fed and that there is no demographic bomb ticking away, while still insisting that there are 'reasons for worry about the long-term effects of population growth on the environment'.[5] The aim of this chapter is to examine the claim that population growth represents a danger to the environment. In particular, it will attempt to determine whether there is a link between population growth and environmental degradation.

8.1 Reinventing Malthus

The contemporary belief that population growth threatens the environment is often linked to a more long-standing argument about resources. In some respects it represents an elaboration of the original Malthusian thesis. The traditional Malthusian view-point was that shortages of land, minerals and other basic resources were the cause of economic slow-down, poverty and malnutrition. In the newer, contemporary version of this argument, population growth is said to threaten the environment itself, or 'the earth's life-supporting resources', as the Commission on Global Governance puts it. The emphasis of the old Malthusian framework was on the depletion of resources, or the limitations of resource bases. The emphasis of the new Malthusian framework is on `soils losing fertility or being eroded'; 'polluted air and water'; and `climate change and ozone depletion', to list but three of the changes to the environment which are said by the Commission to `make the earth less habitable and life more hazardous' (p. 29).

In contemporary texts on environment and population, it is common to find both the old and the new Malthusian arguments deployed. For the purposes of this chapter, the two themes are considered separately. The older Malthusian synthesis is considered first.

The impossibility of food production keeping up with population growth was the central motif of Malthus' *Essays*. This view, regarding environmental constraints on a growing population, has continued to inspire contemporary neo-Malthusians. The durability of Malthus' appeal is all the more curious, since his predictions have been consistently contradicted by experience. Many subsequent advocates of the population–environment synthesis minimize the significance of this historical experience and argue that while Malthus' views did not correspond to events in the past, they have become relevant today. Since the days of Malthus, one generation of his supporters after another have adopted the same procedure. They contend that some unforeseen development, which Malthus could not foresee, has temporally allowed societies to evade the consequences of his prediction. They then go on and claim that these unforeseen developments only provide a temporary respite from the Malthusian dilemma.

There are many different variants of this attempt to rescue Malthus. 'It is nothing to the discredit of Malthus' doctrines that he did not foresee certain social transformations', wrote the American sociologist, Edward Ross back in 1907. According to Ross, developments like democracy and the emancipation of women have acted as a 'preventive check' on population growth.[6] Others have stressed more economic factors, such as the discovery of the New World, as the explanation why European societies evaded the Malthusian trap. This was the view of William Vogt, one of the first major proponents of the population-environment synthesis. His *Road to Survival* (1949), which strongly influenced leading contemporary writers like Ehrlich, sought to rescue the reputation of Malthus. 'It is perhaps, not strange that the theories of Robert Thomas Malthus were buried beneath the bounty from the New World cornucopia', wrote Vogt (1949, p. 63). Here, the availability of plentiful resources from the New World is the explanation for the 'delay' in the working out of the Malthusian dynamic.

Many writers followed the approach adopted by Vogt. They suggested that European expansion led to the discovery of new cheap food supplies, which allowed Western societies to evade the destructive consequences of population growth. They add that this expansion has now come to an end and that it is only a matter of time before Malthus' predictions are vindicated. Overbeek wrote that there are 'no other "uninhabited" areas left' and that 'it does not seem fit to judge Malthus and his ideas by the hundred years which followed the publication of the "Essay"' (1974, p. 47).

A parallel theme is the claim that technological innovation has, like the search for open spaces, also run its course. Whereas in the past, technological innovation helped postpone Malthus' predicted famine, today, so the argument goes, we face impending disaster because there are no significant innovations left in the scientist's locker.

In *Full House: Reassessing the earth's population carrying capacity* (1995), Lester Brown and Hal Kane of the Worldwatch Institute, combine the motif of diminishing technological innovation with the theme of no more virgin territories, and reach this bleak prospect: 'From mid-century until recently, grain output projections were for the most part simple extrapolations of trends. The past was a reliable guide to the future. But in a world of limits, this is changing' (pp. 23–4). Brown and Kane's text provides a shopping-list of post-Malthus environmental 'limits' and concludes on a typically anti-natalist tone:'the bottom line is that achieving a humane balance between people and food supplies may now depend more on family planners than on fishers and farmers' (p. 202).

Those who affirm the relevance of old Malthusian arguments can at times be cavalier with the facts. Their results follow from Malthusian assumptions which bear little relation to reality. Typically they are driven by the intuition that circumstances must change for the worse. At a South African conference on population growth in 1970, the dogmatic quality of this intuitive discourse was vividly confirmed. According to Professor Marcus Arkin 'the operation of Malthus' law had been allayed by various factors' but 'it would be wrong to say that it had been disproved'. Here was a law that did not function but which for some reason could not be 'disproved'. Ugo Papi, an Italian demographer in attendance, was prepared to accept that Malthus' reasoning was 'defective', but nevertheless, contended that 'his intuition is still full of significance for us'. Others were more down to earth; the American demographer, Joseph Spengler took the view that the measures taken to prevent food shortages created an environmental cost. As environmental costs mounted, Malthus' predictions would be vindicated (see Barratt and Louw, 1972, pp. 37, 38 and 73).

One way around the perennial failure of Malthusian predictions has been to accept that there is sufficient food in the here and now, but to raise doubts about the ability of the earth to feed itself in the indefinite future. Harrison adopts this approach: 'So far so good. But we cannot safely extrapolate the past into the future. There have been food crises in the past. In Africa there are recurrent food crises in the present. No one can guarantee that there will be none in the future' (1993, p. 42). Harrison is prepared to project demographic problems into the future but not the ability of human beings to adapt to their circumstances. According to this intellectual double standard, it is permissible to project the problems into the future, but not the solutions! Brown and Kane similarly adopt as an assumption the hypothesis that 'there will be no dramatic technological breakthroughs that will lead to quantum jumps in world food output comparable to those associated with the discovery of fertilizer, the hybridization of corn, or the development of the high-yielding dwarf wheats and rices' (1995, p. 162). This approach is directly borrowed from the method deployed by Malthus, according to which it is assumed that every form of technical progress in agriculture is a temporary tendency whereas the law of diminishing return is significant for all times.

The counter argument to those who renounce the possibility of future technological innovation does not depend on naive expectations of technical and scientific inventions as yet unforseen. It is not a matter of upholding Dr Pangloss against the Malthusian Cassandras, as is often thought.[7] Existing best practice could produce more than enough food for many times the current population of the world. Today, as the food mountains attest, the ability of the Earth to support its human inhabitants is not in question. We already produce enough food to feed our current population, plus another thirty per cent.[8] Moreover, half the available land in the world, which could be cultivated quite productively, is not yet farmed. As for soil degradation, it is not a consequence of over-use, but rather of economic policies and thus bad agricultural practices. In large parts of the South, sheer economic plight drives people to mine the land.

Given the right social and economic arrangements, African land could be farmed five times more intensively than it is. This level of intensive farming already exists in America, yet America suffers far less degradation of its soil than does Africa. The potential for increased food production is held back by the prevailing forms of socio-economic organization and not by the limits of nature. It has been estimated that, using agricultural techniques already in existence, the South alone could feed 32 billion people; and that is without the contribution of the vast fertile areas of Russia and the Ukraine (see Harrison, 1993, p. 46).

These facts are quoted by Harrison, who runs through the enormous documentary evidence showing the gap between the promise and the reality of Third World agriculture (pp. 43–5). But he refuses to base his policy prescriptions on that promise. Instead he assumes that each country must feed itself, and then only with existing levels of technology and skill. As with the perception that things must change for the worse, this localist assumption necessarily leads to Malthusian conclusions. Despite the existence of a long-standing international division of labour, Harrison and his co-thinkers uphold Malthus and claim that each nation state must grow all its own food or be condemned to oblivion.

The old Malthusian arguments, while still popular, are too easily challenged to serve as a reliable environmental justification for the population control lobby. During the seventies these ideas were elaborated and supplemented with new insights. This project of reinventing Malthus required that at least his central concern with diminishing food supplies should be downplayed. Despite the warnings of Ehrlich and his collaborators, the world suffered from a surplus of food rather than a shortage. As a recent United Nations report pointed out, the real price of food continues to fall and future population growth is unlikely to reverse this trend (1994, p. 230). The false expectation of food shortages was at the level of empirical reality the Achilles Heel of the Malthusian perspective. Those who were attached to anti-natalist concerns found it difficult to concede that Malthus was wrong about the problem of food, without elaborating an alternative way of rationalizing population policy. Writing in this vein, Gerhard Heilig has accepted that 'there is no foreseeable limitation to the basic natural resources of food production'. Nevertheless, he still demanded 'better arguments' to 'convince people that global food production may be limited'.[9]

The 'better' arguments sought by Heilig need to account for the failure of Malthus' predictions whilst offering a new variant of the population–environment synthesis. One such argument is provided by the American ecologist C. S. Holling. According to Holling, there were two reasons why Malthus' prediction about the collapse of the earth did not materialize. First, the natural ecological system has proved to be resilient. Second, human creativity has overcome the obstacles it encountered, human beings have been able to 'create and innovate when limits are reached'. So can this state of affairs continue indefinitely? Holling warned against such optimistic conclusions. To justify this stance, he noted that the resilience of natural systems is not unlimited and that people's 'adaptive and creative abilities rely on specific contexts set by the environment'. For Holling the balance between people and nature has become precarious since for the first time, 'humanity and nature are transforming each other on the whole planet'.[10] This argument is based on the intuition that as the scale of the interaction between people and the environment increases, the existing balance is threatened.

Ecologists like Holling have succeeded in presenting a theory which accounts for the failure of Malthus' predictions, while retaining the core argument about the danger of population growth. In this version of the argument, population growth threatens to destroy the balance between people and the environment, in the indefinite future. In the more sophisticated theories, there is a reluctant acceptance of the proposition that there is no food or resource problem, it is the ecological balance which represents the new limit. Paul Harrison's *The Third Revolution* (1993) offers a well-argued account of this perspective.

Harrison accepts that events have not been kind to Malthus' views: 'Over the past two centuries, Malthus' basic theorem has been turned upside down. Human ingenuity has so far been able to increase world food production in line with the increase in human numbers' (1993, p. 42). He acknowledges the role of human creativity and is prepared to concede that there is sufficient food to feed people. However, like Holling he is pessimistic about the effectiveness of human ingenuity in the future. According to Harrison the frontier is closing down, there is nowhere for people from overcrowded regions to go. Worse still, the growth in population will inexorably lead to an environmental catastrophe. The focus of the argument has dramatically shifted from an old-fashioned Malthusian famine to a crisis which, according to Harrison, is 'broader' than anything hitherto envisaged. 'It is not a resource crisis but a pollution crisis', wrote Harrison. And in apocalyptic tone he adds that 'life may survive in some lowly form' but 'we may not' (pp. 53–4).

The new Malthusian thesis as presented by Harrison, is a novel development in the argument. In response to fairly effective critiques of traditional Malthusian themes (see, for example, Simon, 1981 and 1986; Allaby, 1995; and North, 1995), old Malthusians such as Ehrlich and Brown have climbed aboard this more successful train of thought. They expand the scope of the problem, so that virtually every form of human activity becomes a contribution to pollution. Every possible peril, from AIDS to global warming is mobilized to justify the case for population control. Harrison, Ehrlich and Brown have little to say about the dynamics of population growth. What they have done is to fuse the population variable with wider environmental concerns. More specifically, population growth is represented as the main determinant of environmental degradation. Whereas in previous decades, population growth was held responsible for poverty, it is now increasingly held accountable for a different problem, that of the environment. In this version of the Malthusian world view, population growth emerges as a pollutant. Every human being is a potential polluter.

One consequence of the theory of people as pollutants is that everyone becomes equally responsible for the degradation of the environment. From this perspective, agricultural communities are no less guilty than the highly industrialized societies of the West, poor cultivators in Africa no less culpable than multi-billion dollar Western enterprises. Whereas in the past poverty was condemned because it degraded people, in the ecological version of Malthusianism poverty is indicted because of its harmful impact on the environment. Poverty is seen as the direct or indirect cause of environmental degradation.[11]

The shift from famine to pollution is the dominant motif in the reincarnation of Malthus. This shift represents a pragmatic accommodation to contemporary reality. As Betsy Hartmann noted, the old arguments about diminishing food supplies have been refuted by the experience of the eighties. At the same time concern with the environment remained in vogue. 'It will be interesting to see if the environmental argument against population growth, like the hunger argument, also passes out of fashion' observed Hartmann (1987, p. 23). It seems likely that the population–environment synthesis is likely to endure for some time. Through this link, Malthus has been given a new lease of life. This is a formidable theme, with tremendous potential to excite the imagination. In their capacity as pollutants, human beings represent a danger not only to themselves but to the entire eco-system.

8.2 The Link between Population and the Environment

The presentation of the population–environment synthesis is based on the assumption that the greater the number of people, the greater the intensity of pressure on the environment. Often this relationship is presented as a self-evident proposition. 'More people, at a given level of per capita consumption, means more pressure on land, food energy and a wide variety of other environmental resources', according to a report on the Rio Summit (Grubb et al., 1993, p. 30). According to this formula, population growth by definition tends to intensify every identifiable environmental problem.

On closer inspection, the confidently asserted linkages between population growth and environmental degradation prove to be far from clear. In many respects, this argument proves to be strikingly similar to previous attempts to present demographic growth as a problem of economic development. In particular, the population–environment synthesis has little in the way of empirical validation.

As with the narrative on economic development, case studies are invariably more neutral about the link between population and the environment than are the more propagandist texts. Here are some examples.

John Clarke, who is concerned with raising awareness about global environmental issues, has noted that the 'controversy over the interrelationship between population and environment has not been based upon a great deal of research'.[12] The absence of systematic research has not proved a barrier to those determined to blame environmental problems on population growth. 'The paucity of research has not, unfortunately, slowed down popular or even academic writing on the policy implications of presumed population–environment linkages', wrote Gita Sen (Sen, Germain and Chen, 1994, p. 69). A review of the literature on land degradation and population change found that the various theories were rarely substantiated by empirical evidence. It added that 'many of the assumptions underlying these theories have yet to be proven.'[13]

Some contributors openly acknowledge that their concern regarding the link between population growth and environmental degradation is based on guess work rather then empirical investigation. The lack of hard evidence does not in any way inhibit them from vigorously advocating their case. Stephen Lonergan explained his position in the following terms: 'One conclusion reached by Holmberg, and seconded by the present author, is that detailed empirical studies of these relationships are woefully lacking and, in the absence of such studies, only anecdotal evidence and intuitive judgements can be used to assist in understanding the linkages amongst poverty, population growth and environmental degradation.'[14] Intuition requires little in the way of justification. Thus neither Lonergan nor his co-thinkers make any attempt to justify why they assume the prior existence of the population–environment linkage. Lonergan notes that due to the 'paucity of empirical work' the 'complexity and controversy surrounding the linkages are somewhat oppressive', but does not hesitate to assume the existence of the linkages.[15] That which has yet to be proved, constitutes the intuitive foundation for the argument.

The flood of literature promoting the population-environment synthesis, despite the absence of empirical evidence, suggests that it may well also be ideologically driven. The dogmatic character of this argument came to the surface during a heated encounter between Ehrlich and his fellow environmental activist, Barry Commoner. Ehrlich wanted to suppress Commoner's conclusion in his book *The Closing Circle*, which argued that pollution rather than population was the greater cause of damage to the environment. Commoner concluded 'Ehrlich is so intent upon population control as to be unwilling to tolerate open discussion of data that might weaken the argument for it' (cited in Bailey, 1993, p. 53).[16] Ehrlich has no monopoly on dogma; Paul Demeny was also disturbed by the implications of Commoner's work. His response to Commoner's book illustrates a dogged determination to uphold the population–environment synthesis.

Demeny conceded that Commoner had a point about the impact of technology and of Western consumption on the environment. But he insisted that numbers of people were still critical to the equation. He observed:

> Accepting the premise that resource and environmental problems are caused by a concatenation of factors among which population is only one does not, however, relegate the demographic component to a rank of 'also rans'. The notions of 'resources' and 'environment' make sense only in relation to human numbers: concern with the relative scarcity of 'goods' compared to people is the underlying rationale for most examinations of resource and environmental issues.[17]

Once the problem is defined in this form – where resources are *a priori* scarce and fixed relative to people – population becomes the only variable that can make any difference, since it is seen as the only one that is not fixed. In this way, the population–environment synthesis becomes self-defined; a fact of nature.

The character, and defects, of the argument can be understood through a study of Paul Ehrlich's famous formula, IPAT.

Impact = Population × Affluence × Technology

According to this formula the impact of a population on the environment is the product of the size of the population (P), its level of affluence (A), and the impact of the technologies (T) that sustain the level of affluence. The implication of this formula is straightforward – the more people there are, the more they consume, and the more technology they use, the greater the damage to the environment.

But what is impact? The term suggests that human impact brings about changes to the environment which are harmful and destructive to life. So impact means erosion of land, for example. Taking erosion as a test case, is there any evidence that more people, more consumption, and more technology leads to more erosion? The size of population, the degree of affluence and the technology deployed does not reveal very much about the dimensions of damage caused to the environment. Populations do not behave in a homogeneous way. Their relationship to nature is mediated through different social organizations and technologies. Consequently some groups contribute to and change their environment whilst others are primarily involved in consumption. What impact particular groups of people make on the environment cannot be deduced through a technical formula in advance. It needs to be studied in its specificity.

Consider, first of all, affluence and technology. The comparison made earlier in this chapter between erosion of land in Africa and America counts against the claim that more of either or both of affluence and technology is destructive: African land is farmed using a lower level of technology, and levels of consumption are much lower than in America. And yet, on average, erosion is much higher in Africa than it is in America. The reason is simple – economic pressures force many Africans to ignore the basics of soil science. Soil is a combination of crushed rocks, minerals, water and organic matter. There is no limit to its ability to produce food if these elements are replenished, and the soil is not poisoned. Soil will replenish itself if a variety of crops are farmed on it, and it is left fallow for a period. Alternatively, it can be replenished using fertilizers. Monocropping, often for export, combined with overuse to meet immediate need without sufficient use of fertilizer, is the cause of the higher levels of erosion in Africa in comparison with America.

What of population? The coexistence of environmental problems with a particular level of population does not necessarily imply a causal relationship between the two. The degradation of the environment may well be the outcome of the action of a small number of individuals who are involved in the exploitation of certain resources without regard to the social consequences of their action. Or it may be the result of the actions of large numbers of poor cultivators, who lack the resources to manage their land.

From the available evidence, it is possible to argue that environmental problems can coexist with a low density of population as well as with a high density. Famine and soil erosion in countries like Ethiopia, the Sahel or Tanzania has little to do with high population density. A collection of case studies from Africa published in the early nineties found it difficult to establish a clear relationship between levels of population and the environment.

Some of the case studies suggested that rapid population growth had a positive impact on the environment, whilst others concluded that it led to the degradation of the land. The editors of these studies concluded that 'degradation of a severity that destroys agriculture does not necessarily follow from the high population pressures or intensive cultivation' (Turner et al., 1993, p. 409).

In some cases, it is not so much population growth but depopulation which is associated with environmental degradation. According to Janice Jiggins, this is what happened in parts of Nepal, where the depopulation of the mountainsides through migration had a damaging impact on the environment. There were not enough people to maintain agricultural terraces, replant trees and carry on the practices that have sustained mountain agriculture in the past.[18] The Nepalese experience illustrates the importance of human labour in the establishment of a creative balance between society and nature. Contrary to the Ehrlich IPAT formula, it suggests that in some cases, it may be the *lack* of human impact which is responsible for environmental destruction.

The Malthusian standpoint on the relationship between population and the environment has been challenged on a number of significant points. Ester Boserup's important study *The Conditions of Agricultural Growth* (1993) argues a thesis which is in many respects the opposite to that of Malthus. According to Boserup, population growth has historically stimulated agricultural development, which on balance had a positive impact on the environment. She believes that population growth has played a creative role, leading to the intensification of agriculture. 'I have reached the conclusion' she noted, 'that in many cases the output from a given area of land responds far more generously to an additional input of labour than assumed by neo-Malthusian authors' (p. 14). Boserup has argued that increased demand for food and land shortage stimulates the adoption of techniques which intensify cultivation. These new techniques combined with more labour contribute to a more efficient use of land and lead to a rise in output. Others have argued that population growth stimulates human creativity, boosts the market and provides for efficiencies of scale. Simon, for example has pointed to the advantages of higher population density for reducing the per capita cost of building roads and other infrastructural projects. The cheapening of transportation and the subsequent increase of human interaction enhances the capacity of communities to generate new ideas (see Simon, 1977).

Boserup's hypothesis is supported by an important study of Machakos District in Kenya by Tiffen, Mortimore and Gichuki. The study *More People, Less Erosion* offers a fascinating counterpoint to the traditional Malthusian thesis. Machakos District is densely populated by the Akamba people. As far back as the thirties, Machakos had a reputation as an environmental disaster area. On numerous occasions the area was written off as having no economic potential. And yet today, much of the area has been recovered and the system of agriculture has been reorganized on a profitable basis. The main finding of the authors is that 'population increase is compatible with environmental recovery' so long as it is linked to market opportunities. According to the report a highly efficient but labour intensive system of terracing came into existence in Machakos. The system of terracing helped conserve soil and water and led to an increase in tree cover. This system made it possible to grow high value crops such as coffee and fruits as well as to increase the yield of grains and pulses.

For the authors, the Machakos experience undermines the population–environment synthesis. They argue that with a slower rate of population growth, there might have been 'less labour available for conservation technologies, resulting in less market demand and incentives for investment' (1994, p. 284). Tiffen, Mortimore and Gichuku isolate four positive consequences of population growth. These are: '(A) increased food needs: (B) increased labour supply; (C) increased interaction of ideas leading to new technologies: (D) economies of scale in the provision of social and physical infrastructure' (p. 266). The picture presented here is of a mutually reinforcing process, whereby population pressure stimulates innovation and efficiency. Dense population creates economies of scale for infrastructural initiatives and helps generate new ideas.

The Malthusian approach has also been criticized by those who argue that land degradation and agrarian stagnation are the consequence of a combination of institutional weakness and lack of market incentives. Srinivasan has argued that the so-called resource crisis has been overplayed. He points to the potential for raising output in many parts of the South through the adoption of known superior technology which is already in use elsewhere. He indicts government policies which he claims have 'blunted and distorted the incentives of farmers to enlarge food supplies'. Srinivasan concludes that the main cause of famine is 'not shortages of food or rapid population growth but colossal *policy* failures unrelated to population growth'.[19]

The Machakos experience demonstrates the creativity and adaptability of human beings. However, this experience is not an argument for attaching positive virtues to population growth as such. The intensification of agricultural activities does not depend entirely on high rates of population growth. An important variable influencing intensification and innovation in agriculture is the availability of incentives and market opportunities. Pingali and Binswanger have argued that the intensive production of groundnuts in Senegal, of maize in Kenya and Zambia and of cotton in Uganda have all followed the installation of the railway, and have been concentrated in areas close to the railway line. 'It should be noted,' they add, 'that agricultural intensification in response to improved market access could occur even under low population densities due to individual farmers expanding their cultivated area by including more marketed crops'.[20] The main conclusion to be drawn from the experience of agricultural intensification is the indeterminate character of the relationship between population and the environment.

It is paradoxical that many opponents of the population–environment synthesis adopt a method which is similar to that used by Malthusians. They too isolate population growth as a key variable but instead of attaching negative qualities to it, they endow it with positive significance.[21] So Tiffen and Mortimore argue that 'population density from a low base sets in train processes which can lead to environmental improvement as well as increased incomes per capita'.[22] Why population should be the key variable in this scenario is just as unclear as in the Malthusian framework, which they otherwise criticize.

Agricultural development and environmental well-being is influenced by a complex range of factors. Neither is directly – positively nor negatively – determined by population growth. There are many examples where a low density of population led to a wastage and degradation of land. The French demographer Alfred Sauvy remarked that 'wasting land is usually a feature of not very dense populations'. He had in mind the examples of the Mississippi Valley, Brazil and Madagascar (1969, p. 287). At the same time, a high density of population is not in and of itself a guarantee of a sound system of land management. The wide range of contrasting experiences among different groups of people and their environment must lead to the conclusion that there is no causal relationship – either positive or negative – between population density and the environment.

The population–environment synthesis requires that both sides of the relationship have a fixed and technical quality. It ignores historical experience, which shows that people interact, learn and adapt to their circumstances. People build new institutions, develop new technologies and innovate new practices. Nor does the environment remain static – the physical condition of the earth has always been in a state of change.

The attempt to link population growth to environmental problems is based on the assumption that human induced changes tend to be primarily destructive. It is interesting to note that impact in the IPAT formulation is assumed to have an inexorably negative effect on the environment. Yet experience shows that more people does not mean greater 'impact', if 'impact' means the deterioration of the environment. People can conserve, create and destroy. The consequences of their action are determined by their form of organization and the technology they use.

Some supporters of the IPAT formula are sensitive to its more obvious defects. Harrison seeks to make the formula more precise in his *The Third Revolution*. However, his modification of the formula tends to reveal its underlying incoherence. Earlier it was argued that an increase in any of the terms P, A, T does not necessarily lead to an increase in impact. A careful inspection of each of these terms suggests that the formula is merely tautological. As Harrison noted, affluence can be more precisely defined as consumption per person, or consumption by population. He further argued that the consequence of technological change is measured by impact per unit of consumption, or impact divided by consumption. Plugging these terms into the IPAT formula, we have:

$$I = \text{population} \times \text{consumption}/\text{population} \times \text{Impact}/\text{consumption}.$$

If the right hand side is rationalized, we are left with the formula Impact = Impact, a tautology which reveals nothing about the size of the impact.

In assessing the relevance of the IPAT formula, we have focused on erosion of soil. There are, of course, other issues which concern environmentalists. The most significant are the salination of soil due to irrigation, the poisoning of water due to fertilizer use, and global climate change. Superficially, these issues seem to prove the population lobby's point rather better than does the issue of erosion – after all, the line linking more people, more irrigation, more fertilizer and more poisoning seems clear enough, as does the link between more people and global warming. However, real as these problems are, the use of them to justify a population control agenda is another example of the Malthusian imperative at work.

Lester Brown and Hal Kane emphasize salination and poisoning, as does Harrison. For these authors, the two problems highlight absolute limits to food production. Even if we can feed the world many times over, we cannot do it indefinitely, they say, since doing so means slowly but surely undermining the goose that lays the golden egg – land and water. And, they claim, there is no obvious way out, since there are no scientific solutions on the horizon that could boost output per portion of land, and thus alleviate the problem. Farmers, write Brown and Kane, 'search in vain for new advances, perhaps from biotechnology, that will lift world food output quickly to a new level. But biotechnology has not produced any yield-raising technologies that will lead to quantum jumps in output, nor do many researchers expect it to' (1995, p. 25).

This chapter has already taken issue with the double standard employed by writers such as Brown and Harrison. And this needs emphasizing. Just because new breakthroughs are not visible, it does not mean that they will not occur. Many of the great breakthroughs in science have been unforeseen. Indeed, 'new advances', by their very nature, are often unforeseen, otherwise the advance would have already been made. But there is another, perhaps more telling issue at stake. Even if Brown and Harrison are right to speculate that there are no new biotechnology inventions on the horizon which could boost food production, there are new developments on stream now that will enable the same amount of food to be produced on a given piece of land in ways that cause less poisoning of the soil.

If irrigation is a problem in a particular region because it leads to excessive salination, then the development by Israeli scientists of crops which require less water will be of use. Israel had an incentive to make this advance because of water shortages rather than salinated soils, but the advance, the invention, is there to be used in a different context. If poisoning due to fertilizer use is the problem, then biotechnology inventions currently on stream will be of interest. Ways have been suggested for modifying crops to enable them to fix nitrogen directly from the air. Given that nitrogen is, in water run-offs, one of the more problematic components of fertilizers, this biotechnology invention should be a great help (see HMSO, 1995).

The search for limits seems always to distract Malthusian thinkers from the far more creative search for solutions. The fatalism regarding future innovation reveals that the real limit which preoccupies them is not so much that of land or of resources, but their own limited view of the human potential. This pessimism is combined with a cavalier analytical procedure which declares that all problems facing the environment are by definition associated with the numbers of people. From fears of resource depletion to concerns about erosion, from talk of salination and poisoning to doom-mongering about climate change, the population–environment synthesis is an artificial way of blaming environmental degradation on the numbers of people. By a sleight of hand, it transforms the problem of population into that of the environment. For those who are genuinely concerned with their environment the answer does not lie in population control. With more innovative forms of social organization and technology, conservation measures can be mounted and new approaches found. Only those who are obsessed with population control and searching for an argument to justify it can equate the problem of the environment with demography.

9

Conclusions: Population and Development Discourse – The Parting of the Ways

The previous chapters have reviewed the different dangers which have been associated with population growth through the years. The one constant feature of the discussion of population has been the pragmatic and instrumental manner with which arguments have been deployed. From the early, brief flirtation with development to today's advocacy of gender issues, the sense of tactical expediency within the population lobby is evident. The defining feature of demographic consciousness is its *a priori* assumption that the growth of population is intrinsically a problem. From this perspective, the very term population implicitly is associated with images of danger and threat. Consequently, population is rarely discussed as anything other than a problem.

Statements about demography are often represented as incontrovertible technical facts. But of course, such statements are much more than facts. They involve a process of isolation and selection, as well as exclusion, and finally of interpretation. Most statements about population are actually motivated by a much wider agenda. For example, many of the debates at the Cairo Conference and in its aftermath were a direct spin-off of the clash of views about abortion and family values in the United States and other parts of the West. Arguments conducted in Western newspapers about the effects of population growth were strongly influenced by the protagonists' attachments in the abortion debate.[1] Some of the most forceful critics of the population lobby are influenced by the so-called religious right movement. From their perspective, population policies are merely a variant of what they perceive to be a crusade against the traditional family led by liberals and feminists.[2] Here, population policy has become another battlefield on which a wider ideological war is fought.

The debate on abortion is only one of the underlying themes that shape the population controversy. Traditional geopolitical concerns still influence demographic consciousness. Many of the most alarmist interventions on this subject have been inspired by strategic concerns regarding migration and global instability. On the other side of the debate, a significant proportion of the small group of vocal opponents of population policies are strongly driven by their free-market and anti-state intervention philosophies.

As noted previously, statements about population are intimately linked to a preoccupation with power, race and nation. The motif of differential or competitive fertility is rarely acknowledged. Nevertheless it remains close to the surface. The absence of any major public discussion of competitive fertility is a testimony to significant silences in the literature on demography. It also signifies the tension between the population lobby's real agenda and the rhetoric it employs within the demographic discourse. The population lobby has consistently sought to distance itself from its openly eugenic past. It is sensitive to the charge of racism and has attempted to forge a more enlightened image. Consequently, a lot of anxieties connected with demographic consciousness are only openly expressed in the non-specialist literature. Issues like immigration, political instability or the threat from competing races are studiously avoided at international conferences on population.

The tension contained within the agenda of population control is expressed through a permanent search for effective arguments. Lack of confidence in the presentation of the case has shifted the focus to the packaging of population policies. Population policies are rarely marketed in explicitly demographic terms these days. The tendency is to integrate population policies into other more neutral programmes such as health care, education and the empowerment of women. The words used to package population policies are chosen with care. So often policies which are designed to reduce fertility are represented as giving women more choice. Donald Warwick has drawn attention to the cultivation of an inoffensive vocabulary used to market policies: 'Those who favour fertility control prefer the phrase family planning, which has overtones of rationality, self-direction, and human welfare, rather than birth control, which implies limits on free choice. Linguistic euphemisms are particularly common in debates about abortion. Those in favour call themselves pro-choice rather then pro-abortion; those opposed, pro-life rather than anti-abortion' (in Finkle and McIntosh, 1994, p. 190). It is difficult to avoid the conclusion that the vocabulary associated with population issues is designed to mystify rather than clarify.

The linguistic acrobatics of the population lobby are symptomatic of an underlying defensiveness. As this book has indicated, the population lobby is continually in search of new arguments. If an argument is lost or becomes embarrassing, Malthusians have no inhibitions about distancing themselves from it. So Hardin, the hardline Malthusian, has complained that the 'practical issue of population control' has become 'entangled with the moral issue of abortion'. As far as Hardin is concerned, if support for abortion rights weakens the cause of population control, then it should be dropped. 'Limiting population growth is easier to achieve when abortion is readily available, but population control is quite possible in a nation that prohibits abortion', he wrote (1993, p. 4). Such pragmatism towards ideas leads to a continuous reworking of the arguments for population control.

Those who advocate population policies are rarely explicit about their objectives. Recent appeals to the cause of redistribution, the empowerment of women or the defense of the environment self-consciously sidestep the issue of numbers. Such reactions express an anxiety about open association with population control. Indeed publications on the subject continually protest that the reduction of numbers is only one component of their reproductive health package.

9.1 Who is Planning Whose Family?

The tension between the objective of reducing the rate of fertility and the attempt to present this goal in the language of choice remains unresolved. This is not surprising since it is the motive of controlling fertility, and not the desire to offer choice in the abstract, which has inspired population policy. Those who market population control are particularly sensitive to the charges of coercion. Exposés of coercive practices in Bangladesh, China, Indonesia and India have undermined the confidence of many family planning practitioners. Some have genuinely sought to find alternatives to what they consider to be unacceptable coercive practices. Some believe that more sensitive and structured interventions can reconcile both the 'societal goals of a reduced rate of growth and individual goals of desired and healthy reproduction'. In this way 'the legitimacy of population policies' which are conceived 'in full respect of individual rights' is upheld.[3]

In practice the objectives of stabilizing the population and defending individual rights are not so easily reconciled. Population programmes attempt to resolve this tension by influencing attitudes towards fertility through education and other indirect means. Such indirect approaches avoid the worst excesses of coercive programmes. However, such approaches by definition attempt to change attitudes and practices and seek acquiescence rather than dialogue. This relationship is more comparable to that between parent and child than one between equal partners. In this relationship between those who know best and those who are ignorant of vital population issues, there is always the implication of coercion.

Population policies do not merely disseminate information. They involve influencing and shaping behaviour. Riedmann's study of fertility surveys in Africa has shown that they systematically promoted moral lessons. Such lessons sought to uphold the moral superiority of the Western nuclear family and influence the reproductive behaviour of the respondents. According to Riedmann, any changes in reproductive behaviour 'are not indications simply of *cultural diffusion* but the results of core-controlled *cultural imposition*' (1993, p. 109). Anyone familiar with the dynamic of interaction between an international agency and a small rural community will grasp the enormous pressure that will be exerted on the local people. The implication of this dynamic was clearly avoided by Tony Baldry, British Parliamentary Undersecretary for Foreign and Commonwealth Affairs. When asked what constituted coercive population control, he replied: 'Population activities would be considered coercive if they sought to infringe the basic right of couples and individuals to decide freely and responsibly the number and spacing of their children'.[4] Since population programmes are designed to reduce fertility, their aim is not to provide free choice but to influence people towards a particular outcome. A village where people 'freely' decided to increase their rate of fertility would not be considered a success by those in charge of a population project. The pressure is clearly in one direction – and the line between pressure and coercion is in practice blurred.

The unequal relationship between the international population lobby and its target audience in the villages of Africa and Asia was vividly brought home to me while listening to a television news broadcast in Zambia on the night of 2 June 1995. The news item concerned a group of Angolan refugees living in the Mayeba Refugee Camp in the North-western Province of Zambia. Assuming a tone of incredulity, the newscaster reported that the leaders of the refugees had rejected a population programme designed to curb their numbers. They maintained that their people had lost many lives in recent years and that their concern was to replenish their numbers rather then to curb them. The news item concluded on an ominous note 'it is reported that in Mayeba, family planning advice is ignored'. The tone and presentation of this item invited moral condemnation. It suggested that those who ignored the well-meaning expert advice of population campaigners were accomplices in their own downfall. Here was a moral lesson about a misguided community broadcast to the rest of Zambia. It provided a striking illustration of how the 'rights' and 'choices' of ordinary people are represented in the media.

The language of rights was prevalent at the International Conference on Population and Development (IPCD) held at Cairo in September 1994. According to the United Nations Population Fund (UNFPA) report on the conference, 'human rights' were placed at the centre of the discussion. It noted that population stabilization 'can be achieved only by taking individual people's perspectives into account' (1995, p. 2). It also accepted 'the basic human right of all couples and individuals to decide freely and responsibly the number and spacing of their children' (p. 9). However, virtually the whole of the report was not so much about accepting 'people's perspectives' as about how to change them. The authors of the report appeared to be unaware of the contradiction between accepting people's rights to reproduce according to their preference and lecturing them about 'responsible' behaviour.

This contradiction between the rhetoric of rights and the reality of pressure is even more clearly expressed in a recent World Bank study of the impact of education on the fertility of African women. The report concedes that there is little 'unmet need' for contraception in Africa since the 'most recent demographic surveys' indicate that 'women's "ideal family size" ranges from six to nine children per woman'. However, instead of accepting the African 'people's perspectives' on the subject, the report advocates a 'multi-faceted strategy to lower demand for children and raise contraceptive use' (Ainsworth, Beegle and Nyamele, 1995, p. 1). Clearly the concept of unmet need in this case has little to do with meeting the aspirations of African women. More likely, what is at stake is the unmet need of population planners for African clients.

Most studies of fertility practices do not take the views of their subjects seriously. If their investigation reveals a general preference for large families, they have no hesitation in assuming responsibility for changing people's attitudes. Studies of 'unmet need' for contraception are quite open about the fact that their aim is to make people aware of this need, whether they like it or not. Family planning programmes contain an important focus on propaganda. Bongaarts and Bruce, two leading experts working with the Population Council, advocate not just providing family planning services, but also changing attitudes on the issue. They argue that 'an effective program is frequently one that goes far beyond the provision of family planning and contraceptive services by addressing social obstacles to use, such as fear of side effects and social or familial disapproval'.[5] Bongaarts and Bruce are so convinced about their cause that they never pause to ask who gave them the right to tell others how to live, to undermine what they euphemistically refer to as the 'psychological and cultural barriers' to contraception in an African or Asian society.

For family planners the cultural norms and values of target societies are obstacles that need to be overcome through a variety of techniques. Central importance is attached to encouraging women to adopt aspirations, lifestyles and identities which are at variance with the prevailing norms of their societies. 'To reduce unwanted sexual contact and pregnancy, we must assist girls to envision future identities apart from sexual, marital and mothering roles' argue Bongaarts and Bruce'.[6] The far-reaching implications of this perspective of social engineering in developing societies are rarely spelled out. This attempt to foster new aspirations and identities systematically undermines the moral foundation of the target society. Whether societies have a capacity to absorb the effects of such changes is an issue that is simply evaded by the proponents of the new morality.

Population control literature contains an implicit – sometimes explicit – moral condemnation of the culture of fertility that prevails in target societies. It contains a clear assumption of moral superiority, which is expressed routinely in the condemnation of practices deemed to be unacceptable. UNFPA's *The State of World Population* contains a catalogue of practices and beliefs which are confidently dismissed as unacceptable. The report sometimes assumes the tone of a lecture, which runs through a list of practices that should be abolished and another of those which ought to be adopted. Female circumcision is represented as a 'major public health issue'. The need for later marriages is stressed because of its beneficial effect on the rate of population growth. The report advocates western-type male participation in pregnancy, and sex education for young people. Adopting the tone of moral superiority, it lists a series of practices in a manner which invites the reader to react with obvious horror. For example: 'For the women of the Bariba tribe in Benin, having babies is a test of will. Enduring labour and childbirth alone and in silence is a sure route to social respect. Asking for help is considered a sign of weakness and shameful. As a result, many women who could have easily been saved die of complications during delivery' (1995, p. 45). The idea that concepts of shame and respect might be bound up with a sense of dignity and integrity of a people is not even entertained. From the tone of the report, there is the expectation that civilized readers will demand that the Bariba change their standards about respect and shame in the interests of health.

That many of these practices have existed for hundreds of years, that they are integral to the moral and social code of the societies concerned, and that these societies ought to have an opportunity to determine their lifestyle, is paradoxically ignored by a publication which continually advertises the importance of human rights. For all their talk of rights, the right of people to live according to the customs and practices that they have evolved over hundreds of years, appears to be one right which population activists can casually reject.

The issue at stake is not whether one approves of a particular idea or practice. There are many practices in all parts of the world which offend different groups of people. The real issue worth considering is from where do a group of population professionals get the authority to decide what is in the best interest of people in societies around the world. The casual manner with which they condemn other people's social practices is only matched by the uncritical way in which they project their own values on to people living under very different circumstances in the Third World. The language of rights is based on the prior assumption that Western professional experts know best what is really in the interests of the people of the villages of India or Uganda. These assumptions are forcefully expressed in one of the key terms of the Cairo consensus – empowerment.

The term empowerment is often used but seldom defined. It carries the vague impression that somehow certain population policies will empower women. When writers attempt to elaborate this concept, its paternalistic assumptions become evident. According to Batliwala, empowerment is not a response to the grass-root demands of women for particular objectives. Instead it seems that empowering takes place when high-minded individuals, who know what is best, raise the consciousness of the women concerned. Batliwala argues that since 'most poor women have never been allowed to think for themselves' , they are unlikely to question the existing state of affairs. Since the demand for change 'does not usually begin spontaneously from the condition of subjugation', it has to be 'externally induced', by forces with a different 'consciousness' and 'awareness' (in Sen, Germain and Chen, 1994, p. 131). Empowerment is what enlightened professionals do to free women, who otherwise are unclear about their true interest. Those who know best empower those who are misguided about their real needs. But what entitles the empowerer to represent the interests of silent poor women?

The rhetoric of rights and empowerment is part of the patronizing outlook that can ignore what it does not like on the grounds that it knows best. The population lobby swear by the importance of rights – except the right to practice customs of which it disapproves. The contradiction between individual rights and the demands of population control is simply not acknowledged. International Commission on Peace and Food (ICPD) documents enthuse about respecting people's rights, by which they mean attitudes that are consistent with the objectives of population stabilization. Those values and attitudes towards fertility which are inconsistent with population stabilization can be ignored on the grounds that they are not 'responsible' forms of reproductive behaviour.

The cynical manner in which the narrative of demography treats its targets necessitates a critical interrogation of the literature. The question 'what do they really mean?' had to be posed time and again in the previous chapters. A review of the current consensus among population lobbyists, which was arrived at during the Cairo conference, underlines the way the search for a good argument in favour of population control has led to the effective separation of the discussions on demography and development.

9.2 Development and the Cairo Consensus

One of the key ideas pursued through this book is that the relationship of demography to development has always been an instrumental one. Concern about the rate of population growth in the South preceded the elaboration of a developmentalist approach. Indeed, at least in part, the intellectual demand for economic development was motivated by apprehension about the growth of population in Africa, Asia and Latin America. Back in the fifties, development was favoured on the grounds that it would contain rapid population growth. As problems mounted, this perspective was reversed – it was now increasingly suggested that control of population growth was the prerequisite for development. As argued in chapter 4, confusions about this subject gradually weakened the intellectual foundation of the population–development linkage. During the seventies, the developmentalist theme gave way to other motifs in the literature. The stress was now on influencing fertility without development. The arguments shifted back and forth between educating women and citing environmental degradation as the definite population problem. The outcome of this incessant search for an effective rationale for population policies is its separation from the issue of development.

The parting of the ways between population and development discourse can be vividly illustrated through the comparison of two reports published in 1995: the UNFPA's *The State of World Population 1995* and the World Bank's *Global Economic Prospects and the Developing Countries*. These reports have little in common. The UNFPA report says nothing about development. It contains sections on 'The concept of empowerment', 'Safe motherhood' and 'Reproductive tract infections' but does not engage the issue of development. In contrast, the World Bank report,directly addresses the problem of economic development. However, this survey of the prospects of developing societies says nothing about the problem of population. Even a decade ago, both of these organizations displayed a common interest in the relationship between population growth and development.

The population lobby has not entirely dispensed with the

developmentalist agenda. It still finds it useful to issue publicity which links famine and poverty with some population problem. Nevertheless, development has become marginal to the main currents of the contemporary demographic agenda. The term 'development' is often retained in arguments upholding population control. But more out of habit than anything else. So Cairo was formally entitled the International Conference on Population and Development. But the significance attached to the problem of development is demonstrated by the fact that it was only one of six clusters of priority issues identified by the Conference's Preparatory Committee back in March 1991. These issues were: population, environment and development; population policies and programmes; population and women; family planning; health; and family. By the time of the Conference, the issue of development had only the character of a rhetorical afterthought.

Many observers at Cairo, especially from the South were shocked by the disappearance of the issue of development from the population agenda. Even some supporters of the Cairo consensus were uneasy about the marginalization of the problem of development. One account which celebrated the emergence of the 'empowerment of women' as the 'central issue of population policy' was nevertheless disturbed by Cairo's studied silence on economic matters: 'Unfortunately, crucial discussions of economic development were neglected at the ten-day meeting, and environmental concerns were thoroughly ignored. Representatives from southern hemisphere countries, in particular, complained that abortion debates distracted the conference from pressing social and economic issues.'[7] It could be argued that the Conference was not merely 'distracted' but that the new population consensus actually considered the issue of development irrelevant to its mission. Indeed, some of the more hard-line Malthusian publicists have actually become increasingly anti-development. For example, Virginia Abernethy has argued that development may even make the problem of population growth worse. According to her, 'modernization may be the enemy of longterm wellbeing and sustainability, because loss of the traditional culture often leads to higher fertility and rapid population growth' (1993, p. 97).

Supporters of the Cairo consensus have celebrated the way that the conference consolidated a new approach, filling their retrospective conference report with terms like 'landmark consensus' and 'important shift'. Stripped of its rhetorical excess, the new approach in practice means a women-focused strategy. It is based on the conviction that attitudes to fertility can be changed and population growth stabilized, through 'educating' women. As one advocate of this consensus reported: 'the new thinking endorsed in Cairo is that population growth can be stabilized and development efforts enhanced by the advancement of women.'[8] This policy is seen to be the most effective route to the spread of family nuclea- tion and the establishment of a regime of low fertility.

The significance of the Cairo consensus can best be understood if it is placed in the historical context of how the discussion of demography has evolved. This consensus is the outcome of a long and relentless search for a convincing rationale for population control. From past experience, it is difficult to see why the new women-oriented rationale should be any more durable than the development one.

From a historical perspective, the most significant dimension at work in Cairo was the new international balance of power. Back in the seventies, during the proceedings of the Bucharest Conference on population, the nations that constituted the Third World repre- sented a formidable force in global affairs. At Bucharest, the non- aligned movement of Third World countries made a forceful intervention which strongly shaped the population agenda. At the time many Western Malthusians were taken aback by the strength of Third World criticism, and were placed on the defensive. The population lobby never felt comfortable with the conclusion ar- rived at Bucharest, that 'development is the best contraceptive'. One study of the changing trends in American demography has characterized the acceptance of the developmentalist programme at Bucharest as 'a political defeat for the United States'.[9]

Since the end of the Cold War, the influence of non-aligned nations has been significantly reduced. This changing balance of power internationally, in particular the decline of the Third World, cast a long shadow over proceedings at Cairo. In sharp contrast to Bucharest, the agenda at Cairo was shaped by Western interests. Representatives from the South were in no position to bargain and negotiate. The new balance of power has been clearly illustrated by the spread of population programmes in Africa, Asia and Latin America during the nineties. Western pressure to implement popu- lation programmes now meets with far less resistance than in the seventies. Numerous African countries which opposed such poli- cies in the past have now fallen in line. Most countries of the South are now, at the very least, formally committed to promoting population policies.

The pressure to adopt population policies is systemic. Numerous international agencies and non-governmental organizations now insist on the acceptance of anti-natalist policies as a precondition for the granting of aid. Since donors are now in a much stronger position to dictate terms, open resistance to population policy has all but crumbled. Those impoverished societies which hope to receive such aid have no choice but to join the chorus praising population policy. At least this way they have a chance to be 'empowered'.

The irony of course is that the mushrooming of population policies is directly proportional to a declining commitment to the socio-economic transformation of developing societies. In the end-of-the-century imagination, the containment of numbers appears more plausible then socio-economic reform and advance. It seems that, in the New World Order, the weak intellectual underpinning of population control need not be a barrier to the flourishing of demographic consciousness and the conviction that there are too many people.

Notes

Introduction

1 See L. S. Ashford, 'New perspectives on population: Cairo', *Population Bulletin*, vol. 50, no. 1, 1995, p. 31.
2 N. Eberstadt, 'Population change and national security', *Foreign Affairs*, Summer 1991, p. 127.
3 See for example M. King, 'Health is a sustainable state', *The Lancet*, 15 September 1990, p. 665.
4 See also P. Lelouche, 'France in search of security', *Foreign Affairs*, Spring 1993.

Chapter 1 The Numbers Game

1 *Evening Standard*, 31 July 1991.
2 Cited in *The Guardian*, 25 October 1995.
3 See N. B. Ryder, 'Reflections on replacement', *Family Planning Perspectives*, vol. 25, no. 6, 1993 and 'Russian population dropping at alarming rate', *The Globe and Mail*, 7 March 1994.
4 Cited by A. H. Gauthier, 'Towards renewed fears of population and family decline?', *European Journal of Population*, vol. 9, 1993, p. 149.
5 The point about Malthus' objective is well made by P. M. Hauser, 'Present status and prospects of research in population', *American Sociology Review*, vol. 15, 1948, p. 77.
6 See for example R. B. Vance, 'Racial competition for land'. in E. T. Thompson (ed.), Race Relations and the Race Problem (Durham, North Carolina, Duke University Press, 1939) p. 124.

7   E. A. Ross, 'Western civilization and the birth rate', *American Journal of Sociology*, vol. 12, no. 8, 1907, p. 616.
8   E. Grebnik, 'Demography, democracy and demonology', *Population and Development Review*, vol. 15, no. 1, 1989, p. 5.
9   R. D. Kaplan, 'The coming anarchy', *Atlantic Monthly*, February 1994, pp. 46, 49.
10 E. Huntington, 'A neglected tendency in Eugenics', *Social Forces*, vol. 12, no. 1, p. 18 and p. 21.
11 S. Szreter, 'The idea of demographic transition and the study of fertility change: A critical intellectual history', *Population and Development Review*, vol. 19, no. 4, 1993, p. 663.
12 See report in *International Herald Tribune*, 10 October 1995.
13 See P. Lellouche, 'France in search of security', *Foreign Affairs*, Spring 1993, p. 34 and Y. Boyer, 'Demographic change, political priorities and Western security' in L. Freedman and J. Saunders (eds), *Population Change and European Security* (London, Brussey's, 1991), p. 275.
14 B. Lasker, 'Post war migration problems; The far east', *Social Forces*, vol. 221, no. 7, 1943, p. 131.
15 King, 'Health is a sustainable state', *The Lancet*, 15 September 1990, p. 666.
16 See G. McNicoll, 'The agenda of population studies; A commentary and complaint', *Population and Development Review*, vol. 18, no. 3, September 1992, p. 401.
17 D. Hodgson, 'Ideological origins of the Population Association of America', *Population and Development Review*, vol. 17, no. 1, 1991, p. 2.
18 J. R. Wilmoth and P. Ball, 'The population debate in American popular magazines, 1946–90', *Population and Development Review*, vol. 18, no. 4, 1992, p. 651.
19 See *The Observer*, 11 September 1994.
20 N. Eberstadt, 'Book Reviews', *Population and Development Review*, vol. 21, no. 2, 1995, p. 419.
21 See SPUC circular letter, dated 15 November 1994, signed by Alan Rabjohns.
22 The former Marxist historian, Eric Hobsbawn, argues that the two decisive problems facing humanity in the next millennium are 'demographic and ecological'. See E. J. Hobsbawn, *Age of Extremes: the short twentieth century* (London, Michael Joseph, 1994), p. 568.

Chapter 2 Does Population Growth Matter?

1   Allen Kelley and William McGreevey cited in N. Eberstadt, 'Book Reviews', *Population and Development Review*, vol. 18, no. 4, 1992, p. 423.
2   J. Jiggins, 'Don't waste energy on fear of the future', *Conscience*, Autumn 1993, p.27.
3   S. Harper, 'China's population: prospects and policies' in Dwyer (ed.), *China: The Next Decades* (Harlow, Longman, 1994), pp. 67–8.
4   F. Dumont, 'Five lessons in population', *The Catholic World Report*, April 1993, p. 37.

5 See B. Robey, S. O. Rutstein and L. Morris, 'The fertility decline in developing countries', *Scientific American*, December 1993, p. 35.
6 M. Livi-Bacci, 'Population policies: A comparative perspective', *International Social Science Journal*, September 1994, p. 327.
7 Myers, 'Population, environment, and development', *Environmental Conservation*, vol. 20, no. 3, 1993, p. 288.
8 This assumption is questioned by L. Prichett in *Population and Development Review*, vol. 20, March 1994.
9 J. C. Caldwell and P. Caldwell, 'Cultural forces tending to sustain high fertility' in G. T. F. Acsadi, G. Acsadi-Johnson and P. Bulatao, *Population Growth and Reproduction in Sub-Saharan Africa* (Washington DC, World Bank, 1990), p.199.
10 S. Sonko, 'Fertility and culture in sub-Saharan Africa: A review', *International Social Science Journal*, September 1994, p. 397.
11 See J. C. Caldwell and Pat Caldwell, 'High fertility in sub-Saharan Africa', *Scientific American*, May 1990.
12 B. Jewsiewicki, 'Towards a historical sociology of population in Zaire', D. D. Cordell and Gregory J. W. Cordell (eds), *African Population and Capitalism: Historical Perspectives* (Boulder, Colorado, Westview Press, 1987) p. 272.
13 E. Boserup, 'Economic and demographic interrelationships in sub-Saharan Africa', *Population and Development Review*, vol. 1, no. 1 1976, pp. 383–4.
14 R. Evenson, 'Population growth, infrastructure, and real incomes in North India', in R. D. Lee, B. Arthur, A. C. Kelley and T. N. Srinivasan (eds) *Population, Food and Rural Development* (Oxford, Clarendon Press, 1988) p. 120.
15 J. Bongaarts, 'Population policy options in the developing world', *Science*, 11 February 1994, p. 771.
16 J. Bongaarts and J. Bruce, 'The causes of unmet need for contraception and the social content of services', *Studies in Family Planning*, vol. 26, no. 2, 1995, p. 61.
17 'Population growth and our caring capacity', *The Population Council Issues Papers*, 1994, p. 24.
18 Cited in *The Economist*, 28 May 1994.
19 See L. H. Prichett, 'Desired fertility and the impact of population policies', *Population and Development Review*, vol. 20, no. 1, 1994.
20 G. Hardin, 'The tragedy of the commons', in G. A. Love and R. M. Love (eds), *Ecological Crisis: Readings for Survival* (New York, Harcourt Brace Jovanovich, 1970).

Chapter 3 Population and North–South Relations

1 N. Eberstadt, 'Population change and national security', *Foreign Affairs*, Summer 1991, pp. 115–116 and p. 129.
2 P. Lelouche, 'France in search of security', *Foreign Affairs*, Spring 1993, pp. 123–4.

3 See for example O. A. Kokole, 'The politics of fertility in Africa' in J. L. Finkle and C. A. McIntosh (eds), *The New Politics of Population* (New York, The Population Council, 1994).

4 D. R. Chandrasekhar, 'Population problems and international tensions', *International Social Science Journal*, vol. 1, 1949, p. 55

5 See A. H. Gauthier, 'Towards renewed fears of population and family decline?', *European Journal of Population*, vol. 9, 1993, and M. Himmelfarb and V. Baras (eds), *Zero Population Growth: For Whom? Differential Fertility and Minority Group Survival* (Westport, Connecticut, Greenwood Press, 1978).

6 See for example the discussion in Eberstadt, 'Population change', pp. 129–30.

7 *The Guardian*, 12 December 1994.

8 See for example G. D. Foster et al., 'Global demographic trends to the Year 2010: Implications for US security', *The Washington Quarterly*, Spring 1989.

9 Teitelbaum and Winter's work on strategic demography provides many useful insights into how relations of power are experienced through the prism of population in the Western imagination.

10 D. Kirk, 'Population changes and the postwar world', *American Sociological Review*, vol. 9, 1944, p. 32.

11 Chandrasekhar, 'Population problems . . .', p. 61.

12 See E. A. Ross, 'The menace of migrating peoples' in C. H. Turner, *Public Opinion and World Peace* (Washington DC, ILCA, 1923).

13 See for example G. F. McClearey, 'Australia's population problem', *The Milbank Memorial Fund Quarterly*, vol. 20, 1942, p. 32.

14 Sir J. Huxley, 'The world population problem', originally published in 1963, reprinted in G. A. Love and R. M. Love (eds), *Ecological Crisis: Readings for Survival* (New York, Harcourt Brace Jovanovich, 1970), p. 71.

15 K. Sax, 'Population problems' in R. Linton (ed.), *The Science of Man in the World Crisis* (New York, Columbia University Press, 1945), p. 266.

16 See W. B. Vosloo, 'The political implications of the population explosion' in J. Barratt and M. Louw (eds), *International Aspects of Overpopulation* (New York, St Martin's Press, 1972), p. 149.

17 S. J. Holmes, 'The increasing growth-rate of the Negro population', *The American Journal of Sociology*, vol. 42, no. 2, 1936, p. 203.

18 Carnegie Corporation Archives (CCA), *Box 295 Population Investigation Committee*, 'Frederick Osborn to Keppel', 21 May 1937.

19 A. H. Stone, 'Is race friction between blacks and whites in the United States growing and inevitable?', *The American Journal of Sociology*, vol. 13, 1908, p. 18.

20 F. Lorimer, 'Issues of population policy' in P. M. Hauser (ed.), *The Population Dilemma* (Englewood Cliffs, NJ, Prentice Hall, 1969), p. 201.

21 See S. Szreter, 'The idea of demographic transition and the study of fertility change: A critical intellectual history', *Population and Development Review*, vol. 19, no. 4, 1993, for an interesting account of the development of American demographic concerns in this period.

22 E. Charles, 'Population problems in the British overseas dominions', *The Annals*, vol. 237, January 1945, p. 92.

23 Lorimer 'Issues of population policy'.

24 Ibid, p. 195.

25 W. S. Thompson, 'Population prospects for China and Southeastern Asia', *The Annals*, vol. 237, January 1945, p. 79.
26 D. Kirk, 'Population changes and the postwar world', p. 35.
27 On this point, see for example K. Young, 'Population and power', *Social Forces*, vol. 25, no. 1, October 1946, p. 3.
28 K. Davis, 'Population and power' in J. J. Spengler and O. D. Duncan (eds), *Population Theory and Policy: Selected Readings* (Glencoe, Illinois, The Free Press, 1956), pp. 342 and 356.
29 Cited in J. R. Wilmoth and P. Ball, 'The population debate in American popular magazines, 1946–90', *Population and Development Review*, vol. 18, no. 4, 1992, p. 647.
30 See the discussion in chapter 2 of P. J. Donaldson, *Nature Against US: The United States and the World Population Crisis 1965–1980* (Chapel Hill, NC, University of North Carolina Press, 1990).
31 L. Bondestam, 'The political ideology of population control' in L. Bondestam and S. Bergstorm (eds), *Poverty and Population Control* (London, Academic Press, 1980) pp. 11–12.
32 Even as far back as the late forties, this iconoclastic demographer denounced the focus on population control measures in developing societies. He wrote that 'it creates a very disagreeable impression to see people who are white, European, or of European origin, trying to sow the seeds of sterility in populations that are about to escape from under their dominations.' This article 'Le faux problème de la population mondiale', originally published in 1949 is reprinted in *Population and development Review*, vol. 16, no. 4, December 1990, p. 766.

Chapter 4 Forging the Connection between Population and Development

1 See S. Szreter, 'The idea of demographic transition and the study of fertility change: A critical intellectual history', *Population and Development Review*, vol. 19, no. 4, 1993, p. 662.
2 See M. H. Hunt, *Ideology and US Foreign Policy* (New Haven, Yale University Press, 1987), p. 159. This point is also upheld by J. G. Alcade, *The Idea of Third World Development* (Lanham, Maryland, University Press of America, 1987).
3 B. Duden, 'Population' in W. Sachs (ed.), *The Development Dictionary* (London, Zed Books, 1992), p. 151.
4 See for example the Proceedings of the Third Conference of American Lecturers, held in Washington in 1921, in C. H. Turner, *Public Opinion and World Peace* (Washington DC, ILCA, 1923). At this conference, papers on the 'Exploitation of Underdeveloped Areas' and on 'International Migration' anticipated the subsequent themes of the deliberations on development.
5 See J. R. Simpson, 'The origin of United States' academic interest in foreign economic development', *Economic Development and Cultural Change*, vol. 24, 1975–6, pp. 636 and 638.

6 H. W. Singer, 'Economic progress in underdeveloped countries', *Social Research*, vol. 16, 1949, p. 1.
7 K. Davis, 'The world demographic transition', *Annals of the American Academy of Political and Social Science*, 1945, no. 237, p. 10.
8 F. Lorimer, 'Population trends in the Orient', *Foreign Affairs*, vol. 23, no. 4, July 1945, p. 674.
9 S. Chandrasekhar, 'Population growth, socio-economic development and living standards', *International Labour Review*, vol. 69, 1954, p. 540.
10 F. W. Notestein, 'Summary of the demographic background of problems of underdeveloped areas', *The Milbank Memorial Fund Quarterly*, vol. 26, no. 3, July 1948, p. 253.
11 K. Davis, 'Population and the further spread of industrial society'. Published in February 1951, this article is reprinted in J. J. Spengler and O. E. Duncan (eds.), *Population Theory and Policy: Selected Readings* (Glencoe, Illinois, The Free Press, 1956), p. 329.
12 P. M. Hauser, 'Present status and prospects of research in population', *American Sociology Review*, vol. 13, 1948, p. 183.
13 I. H. Taeuber, 'Migration and the population potential of Monsoon Asia', *The Milbank Memorial Fund Quarterly*, vol. 25, no. 1, January 1947, p. 43.
14 See Szreter, 'The idea of demographic transition'.
15 Singer, 'Economic Progress', p. 7.
16 Taeuber, 'Migration and the population potential', p. 31.
17 F. W. Notestein, 'Summary of the demographic background', p. 252.
18 D. Hodgson, 'Demography as social science and policy science', *Population and Development Review*, vol. 9, no. 1, 1983, p. 13.
19 K. Davis, 'Population and the further spread of industrial society', pp. 327–8.
20 F. Lorimer, 'Notes on human fertility in Central Africa' in Milbank Memorial Fund (ed.), *The Interrelations of Demographic, Economic and Social Problems in Selected Underdeveloped Areas* (New York, Milbank Memorial Fund, 1954), pp. 131, 134, 135.
21 P. N. Rosenstein-Rodan, 'The international development of economically backward areas', *International Affairs*, vol. 20, no. 2, 1944, pp. 162, 163.
22 See for example C. Clark, 'Population growth and living standards', *International Labour Review*, August 1953.
23 J. Viner, 'The economics of development', reprinted in A. N. Agarwala and S. P. Singh (eds.), *The Economics of Underdevelopment* (Delhi, Oxford University Press, 1958), p. 9.
24 G. M. Meier, 'The problem of limited economic development', reprinted in Agarwala and Singh, *The Economics of Underdevelopment*, p. 57.
25 H. Mynt, 'The interpretation of economic backwardness', originally published in 1954, reprinted in Agarwala and Singh, *The Economics of Underdevelopment*, pp. 107–8.
26 See P. T. Bauer and B. S. Yamey, *The Economics of Underdeveloped Countries* (Cambridge, James Nisbet and Co., 1957), p. 59 and S. Kuznets 'Toward a theory of economic growth', Published in 1955 and reprinted in S. Kuznets, *Economic Growth and Structure: Selected Esays* (London, Heinemann, 1966), p. 16.

Chapter 5 Development and Population Growth

1 See R. H. Cassen, 'Population and development: A survey', *World Development*, vol. 4, nos 10/11, 1976, p. 806.
2 M. S. Teitelbaum, 'Comment', *World Development*, vol. 4, nos 10/11, 1976, p. 831.
3 P. Demeny, 'Two proposals for the agenda at Cairo', *International Family Planning Perspective*, vol. 20, no. 1, March 1994, p. 30.
4 Eberstadt, 'Book Reviews', *Population and Development Review*, vol. 21, no. 2, 1995, p. 420.
5 Ibid., p. 424.
6 S. Szreter, 'The idea of demographic transition and the study of fertility change: A critical intellectual history', *Population and Development Review*, vol. 19, no. 4, p. 681.
7 T. Thirwall, 'A cross section study of population growth and the growth of output and per capita income in a production function framework', *The Manchester School*, December 1972, p. 341.
8 A. C. Kelley, 'Population pressures, saving, and investment in the Third World: Some puzzles', *Economic Development and Cultural Change*, vol. 36, no. 3, 1988.
9 See for example A. Mason, 'Saving, economic growth, and demographic change', *Population and Development Review*, vol. 14, no. 1, March 1988, p. 113.
10 Sir J. Huxley, 'The world population problem', originally published in 1963, reprinted in G. A. Love and R. M. Love (eds), *Ecological Crisis: Readings for Survival* (New York, Harcourt Brace Jovanovich, 1970), p. 72.
11 See the 1967 paper written by S. Kuznets, 'Population and economic growth', in S. Kuznets, *Population, Capital and Growth: Selected Essays* (New York, W. W. Norton, 1973), pp. 39 and 41; T. Thirwall, 'A cross section study of population growth', p. 352; and R. H. Cassen, 'Population and development', p. 803.
12 For a critique of the methodology deployed in the KAP surveys, see B. Hartmann, *Reproductive Rights and Wrongs: The Global Politics of Population Control and Contraceptive Choice* (New York, Harper and Row, 1987), pp. 58–9.
13 M. S. Teitelbaum, 'Population and development: Is a consensus possible?', *Foreign Affairs*, vol. 52, July 1974, p. 750.
14 J. L. Finkle and B. B. Crane, 'The politics of Bucharest: Population, development, and the new international economic order', *Population and Development Review*, vol. 1, no. 1.
15 Ibid., p. 105.
16 For example see C. A. McIntosh and J. L. Finkle, 'Issues for the future', in J. L. Finkle and C. A. McIntosh (eds), *The New Politics of Population* (New York, The Population Council, 1994), pp. 271–2.
17 See the interesting discussion in M. Nag, 'Economic value and costs of children in relation to human fertility', in Eberstadt (ed.), *Fertility Decline in the Less Developed Countries* (New York, Praeger, 1981).
18 Cassen, 'Population and development', p. 806.

19 M. Perlman, 'Some economic growth problems and the part population policy plays', *Quarterly Journal of Economics*, vol. 89, no. 2, 1975, p. 256.

20 For example, in a recently published collection of essays K. Lindahl-Kiessling and H. Landberg (eds), *Population, Economic Development and the Environment* (Oxford, Oxford University Press, 1994) – no one attempts to argue this point.

21 Cassen, 'Population and development', p. 821.

22 See for example 'Foreword' by Ronald Ridker in R. Repetto, *Economic Equality and Fertility in Developing Countries* (Baltimore, Johns Hopkins University Press, 1979).

23 Cassen, 'Population and development', p. 820.

24 Ridker, 'Foreword', p. xiv.

25 See for example T. Bengsston and C. Gunnarsson, 'Population, development, and institutional change: Summary and analysis' in Lindahl-Kiessling and Landberg, *Economic Equality and Fertility*, p. 21.

Chapter 6 Influencing Fertility: Modernization without Development

1 S. Heschel, 'Feminists gain at Cairo population conference', *Dissent*, Winter 1995, p. 15.

2 See Bengtsson and Gunnarsson, 'Population, development and institutional change', *op.cit*, p. 15 and N. Birdsall, 'Government, population, and poverty: A win-win tale' both in K. Lindahl-Kiessling and H. Landberg (eds), *Population, Economic Development and the Environment* (Oxford, Oxford University Press, 1994), p. 174.

3 N. F. Madulu, 'Population growth, agrarian peasant economy and environmental degradation in Tanzania', *International Sociology*, vol. 10, no. 1, March 1995, p. 42.

4 B. Robey, S. O. Rutstein and L. Morris, 'The fertility decline in developing countries', *Scientific American*, December 1993, p. 34.

5 A. Bandarage, 'Population and development: Toward a social justice agenda', *Monthly Review*, September 1994, p. 46.

Chapter 7 Targeting Women

1 S. A. Cohen and C. L. Richards, 'The Cairo consensus: Population, development and women', *Family Planning Perspectives*, vol. 26, no. 6, November/December 1994, pp. 274–5.

2 Cited in G. S. Smith, 'National security and personal isolation: Sex, gender, and disease in the Cold-War United States', *The International History Review*, vol. 14, no. 2, May 1992, p. 309.

3 E. A. Ross, 'Western civilization and the birth rate', *American Journal of Sociology*, vol. 12, no. 8, 1907, pp. 611, 612 and 616.

4 P. Bachrach, 'The scholar and political strategy: The population case', R. L. Clinton, W. S. Flash and R. K. Godwin (eds), *Political Science in Population Studies* (Lexington, Mass., Lexington Books, 1972) p. 21.

5 S. Johnson, 'Turning the tide', *Geographical*, September 1994, p. 12.

6 See A. Wilson, 'New World Order and West's war on population', *Economic and Political Weekly*, 20 August 1994, p. 2202; and L. Lingham, 'Women, population and development question', *Economic and Political Weekly*, 15 January 1994, p. 85.

7 Anonymous note, 'Politics of population and development', *Economic and Political Weekly*, 17 September 1994, p. 2471.

8 For example in G. Sen, A. Germain and L. C. Chen (eds), *Population Policies Reconsidered: Health, Empowerment and Rights* (Boston, Harvard University Press, 1994), p. 4 the authors touch upon the parallel evolution of women-oriented and structural adjustment policies. They merely describe it as a 'paradox'.

9 'Declaration' by People's Perspectives on 'Population' Symposium, held in Comilla, Bangladesh, 12–13 December 1993.

10 See *The Guardian*, 21 July 1994.

11 A. Bose, 'Gender issues and population change: tradition, technology and social turbulence', *International Social Science Journal*, September 1994, p. 393 and S. Hansen, 'Population: Its challenge to economic and social scientists', *International Social Science Journal*, September 1994, p. 338.

12 See H. Fernandez, 'Persistent inequalities in women's education in Peru' in J. K. Conway and S. C. Bourgue (eds), *The Politics of Women's Education: Perspectives from Asia, Africa and Latin America* (Ann Arbor, University of Michigan Press, 1993), p. 211; and A. Adepoju, 'The demographic profile: Sustained high mortality and fertility and migration for employment' in A. Adepoju and C. Oppong (eds), *Gender, Work and Population in Sub-Saharan Africa*, p. 25.

13 See T. Castro Martin, 'Women's education and fertility: Results from 26 demographic and health surveys', *Studies in Family Planning*, vol. 26, no. 4, 1995, p. 187, for a useful review of the literature.

14 See J. C. Caldwell, 'Fertility in sub-Saharan Africa: Status and prospects', *Population and Development Review*, vol. 20, no. 1, March 1994; and C. Vlassoff, 'Progress and stagnation: Changes in fertility and women's position in an Indian village', *Population Studies*, vol. 46, July 1992, p. 212.

15 J. Cleves Mosse, 'From family planning and maternal and child health to reproductive health' in C. Sweetman (ed.), *Population and Reproductive Rights* (Oxford, Oxfam, 1994), p. 9.

16 A. Sen, 'Population and reasoned agency: Food, fertility, and economic development' in K. Lindahl-Kiessling and H. Landberg (eds), *Population, Economic Development and the Environment* (Oxford, Oxford University Press, 1994), p. 73.

17 P. K. B. Nayar, 'Kerala women in historical and contemporary perspective' in K. Mahadevan (ed.), *Women and Population Dynamics: Perspectives from Asian Countries* (New Delhi, Sage Publications, 1989), pp. 210 and 208.

18 Ibid., pp. 206–7.

19 K. Saradomi, 'Women, Kerala and some development issues', *Economic and Political Weekly*, 26 February 1994, p. 504.

20 R. Savitri, 'Fertility decline in Tamil Nadu: Some issues', *Economic and*

Political Weekly, 16 July 1994, p. 1850.

21 G. McNicoll, 'Review of *Beyond The Numbers*', *Population and Development Review*, vol. 20, no. 3, September 1994, p. 659.

22 L. Hsia, 'Stemming the tide of the global population explosion: The key role of women', *Journal of Nurse-Midwifery*, vol. 40, no. 1, January–February 1995, p. 2.

23 'Empowering women: An essential objective', *UN Chronicle*, September 1994.

24 All references to this document, known as National Security Study Memorandum 200, are taken from *Population Control and National Security; A Review of US National Security Policy*, published by the Information Project For Africa (1991), pp. 3–38.

25 H. J. Wiarda, 'Ethnocentrism and Third World development', *Society*, September/October 1987, pp. 61–2.

26 Cited in Helen Simons, 'Repackaging population control', *Covert Action*, no. 51, Winter 1994–95, p. 36.

27 R. Valenzona, 'The road to Cairo', *Far Eastern Economic Review*, 25 August 1994, p. 21.

28 I. Smyth, '"Safe Motherhood", family planning and maternal mortality: An Indonesian case study' in Sweetman, *Population and Reproductive Rights*, p. 25.

Chapter 8 Environmentalism to the Rescue

1 C. Wichterich, 'From the struggle against "overpopulation" to the industrialization of human production', *Reproductive and Genetic Engineering*, vol. 1, no. 1, p. 24.

2 N. Myers, 'Population, environment, and development', *Environmental Conservation*, vol. 20, no. 3, 1993, p. 209.

3 J. R. Wilmoth and P. Ball, 'The population debate in American popular magazines, 1946–90', *Population and Development Review*, vol. 18, no. 4, 1992, p. 651.

4 G. McNicoll, 'Review of *Beyond the Numbers: A reader on population, consumption and the environment*', *Population and Development Review*, vol. 20, no. 3, September 1994, p. 658.

5 A. Sen, 'Population: Delusion and reality', *The New York Review of Books*, 22 September 1994, p. 71.

6 See E. A. Ross, 'Western civilization and the birth rate', *American Journal of Sociology*, vol. 12, no. 8, 1907, p. 607.

7 See, e.g., Stuart Pimm, 'Cassandra versus Pangloss', *Nature*, 372, pp. 512–13.

8 See J. Seaman, 'Population, food supply, and famine: an ecological or an economic dilemma?' in B. Cartledge (ed.), *Health and the Environment* (London, Oxford University Press, 1994).

9 G. K. Heilig, 'How many people can be fed on earth?' in W. Lutz (ed.), *The Future Population of the World* (London, Earthscan, 1994), p. 236.

10 C. S. Holling, 'Ecologist view of Malthusian conflict' in K. Lindahl-

Kiessling and H. Landberg (eds), *Population, Economic Development and the Environment* (Oxford, Oxford University Press, 1994), pp. 90 and 93.

11 See for example P. Dasgupta, C. Folke, and K. Maler, 'The environmental base and human welfare' in Lindahl-Kiessling and Landberg, *Population, Economic Development and the Environment*.

12 J. L. Clarke, 'Education, population, environment and sustainable development', *International Review of Education*, vol. 39, nos. 1–2, 1993, p. 55.

13 C. L. Jolly, 'Population change, land use, and the environment', *Reproductive Health Matters*, no. 1, May 1993, p. 13.

14 S. C. Lonergan, 'Impoverishment, population, and environmental degradation: The case for equity', *Environmental Conservation*, vol. 20, no. 4, 1993, p. 329.

15 Ibid., p. 328.

16 Commoner now argues that it is production technology rather than population which has the greatest impact on the deterioration of environmental quality. See B. Commoner, 'Population, development, and the environment: Trends and key issues in the developed countries', *International Journal of Health Services*, vol. 23, no. 3, 1993.

17 P. Demeny, 'Demography and the limits to growth' in M. S. Teitelbaum and J. M. Winter (eds), *Population and Resources in Western Intellectual Traditions* (Cambridge, Cambridge University Press, 1989), p. 217.

18 J. Jiggins, 'Don't waste energy on fear of the future', *Conscience*, Autumn 1993, p. 27.

19 T. N. Srinivasan, 'Population growth and food: An assessment of issues, models, and projections' in R. D. Lee, A. C. Kelley and T. N. Srinivasan (eds), *Population, Food and Rural Development* (Oxford, Clarendon Press, 1988), p. 38

20 P. Pingali and H. P. Binswanger, 'Population density and farming systems' in Lee et al., *Population, Food and Rural Development*, p. 54.

21 See for example M. R. Rosenzweig, H. P. Binswanger and J. McIntire, 'From land abundance to land scarcity' in Lee et al., *Population, Food and Rural Development*.

22 M. Tiffen and M. Mortimore, 'Malthus converted: The role of capital and technology in growth and environment recovery in Kenya', *World Development*, June, 1994, p. 997.

Chapter 9   Conclusions: Population and Development
Discourse – The Parting of the Ways

1 For example see the letters page of the London *Times*; 23 May 1995.

2 See for example S. Grimes, 'The ideology of population control in the UN draft plan for Cairo', *Population Research and Policy Review*, vol. 13, no. 3, 1994.

3 See H. Zurayk, N. Younis and H. Khattab, 'Rethinking family planning policy in the light of reproductive health research', *International Social Science Journal*, vol. 14, September 1944, p. 424; and M. Livi-Baci, 'Population policies: A comparative perspective', *International Social Science Jour-*

nal, September 1994, p. 327.

4 See Hansard, 23 May 1995, col. 514.

5 J. Bongaarts and J. Bruce, 'The causes of unmet need for contraception and the social content of services', *Studies in Family Planning*, vol. 26, no. 2, 1995, p. 57.

6 Ibid., p. 72.

7 S. Henschel, 'Feminists gain at Cairo population conference', *Dissent*, Winter 1995, p. 15.

8 L. S. Ashford, 'New perspectives on population: Lessons from Cairo', *Population Bulletin*, vol. 50, no. 1, 1995, p. 2.

9 D. Hodgson, 'Orthodoxy and revisionism in American demography', *Population and Development Review*, vol. 14, no. 4, December 1988, p. 257.

Bibliography

Abernethy, V. D. 1993: *Population Policies: The Choices that Shape Our Future*. New York: Plenum Press.

Acsadi, G. T. F., Acsadi-Johnson, G., Bulatao, D. 1990: *Population Growth and Reproduction Sub-Saharan Africa*. Washington DC: World Bank.

Adepoju, A. and Oppong, C. (eds) 1994: *Gender, Work and Population in Sub-Saharan Africa*. London: James Curry.

Agarwala, A. N. and Singh, S. P. (eds) 1958: *The Economics of Underdevelopment*. Delhi: Oxford University Press.

Ainsworth, M., Beegle, K., and Nyamele, A. 1995: *The Impact of Female Schooling on Fertility and Contraceptive Use*. Washington DC: World Bank.

Alcalde, J. G. 1987: *The Idea of Third World Development*. Lanham, Maryland: University Press of America.

Allaby, M. 1995: *Facing the Future: The Case for Science*. London: Bloomsbury.

Bagehot, W. 1872: *Physics and Politics*. London: Henry S. King & Co.

Bailey, R. 1993: *ECO-SCAM: The False Prophets of Ecological Apocalypse*. New York: St Martin's Press.

Barratt, J. and Louw, M. (eds) 1972: *International Aspects of Overpopulation*. New York: St Martin's Press.

Bauer, P. T. and Yamey, B. S. 1957: *The Economics of Underdeveloped Countries*. Cambridge: James Nisbet & Co. Ltd.

Bondestam, L. and Bergstrom, S. (eds) 1980: *Poverty and Population Control*. London: Academic Press.

Boserup, E. 1993: *The Conditions of Agricultural Growth*. London: Earthscan. Originally published in 1965.

Brown, L. R. (ed.) 1991; *State of the World 1991, A Worldwatch Institute Report on Progress Toward a Sustainable Society*. London: Earthscan.

Brown, L. R. and Kane, H. 1995: *Full House: Reassessing the Earth's Population Carrying Capacity*. London: Earthscan.

Brydon, L. and Chant, S. (eds) 1989: *Women in the Third World: Gender Issues in Rural and Urban Areas*. Aldershot: Edward Elgar.

Calne, R. 1994: *Too Many People*. London: Calder Publications.

Carr, E. H. 1944: *Conditions of Peace*. London: Macmillan.

Carr-Saunders, A. M. 1936: *World Population: Past Growth and Present Trends*. London: Oxford University Press.

Cartledge, B. (ed.) 1994; *Health and the Environment*. London: Oxford University Press.

Clinton, R. L., Flash, W. S. and Godwin, R. K. (eds) 1972: *Political Science in Population Studies*. Lexington, Mass.: Lexington Books.

Coale, A. J. and Hoover, E. M. 1958: *Population Growth and Economic Development in Low-Income Countries*. Princeton, NJ: Princeton University Press.

Commission on Global Governance, 1995: *Our Global Neighbourhood: The report of the Commission on Global Governance*. Oxford: Oxford University Press.

Committee on Population and the Economy, 1994: *Population Information Pack: The Facts about Population Growth*. Richmond, Surrey: Committee on Population and the Economy.

Conway, J. K. and Bourgue, S. C. (eds) 1993: *The Politics of Women's Education: Perspectives from Asia, Africa and Latin America*. Ann Arbor: The University of Michigan Press.

Cordell, D. D. and Gregory, J. W. (eds) 1987: *African Population and Capitalism: Historical Perspectives*. Boulder, Colo.: Westview Press.

Correa, S. 1994: *Population and Reproductive Rights: Feminist Perspectives from the South*. London: Zed Books.

Crocker, W. R. 1931: *The Japanese Population Problem: The Coming Crisis*. London: George Allen & Unwin.

Davis, K. 1951: *The Population of India and Pakistan*. New York: Russell and Russell.

Dixon-Mueller, R. 1993: *Population Policy and Women's Rights: Transforming Reproductive Choice*. Westport, Conn: Praeger.

Donaldson, J. 1928: *International Economic Relations*. New York: Longmans, Green & Co.

Donaldson, P. J. 1990: *Nature Against US: The United States and the World Population Crisis 1965–1980*. Chapel Hill, NC: University of North Carolina Press.

Drakakis-Smith, D. 1992: *Pacific Asia*. London: Routledge

Dwyer, D. (ed.) 1994: *China: The Next Decades*. Burnt Mill, Harlow: Longman.

Eberstadt, N. (ed.) 1981: *Fertility Decline in the Less Developed Countries*. New York: Praeger.

Ehrlich, P. R. 1971 *The Population Bomb*. London: Pan Books. Originally published in 1968.

Ehrlich, P. R. and Ehrlich, A. H. 1970: *Population, Resources, Environment*. San Francisco: W. H. Freeman and Co.

Engelman, R. and Roy, P. 1993: *Conserving Land: Population and Sustainable Food Production*. New York: Population Action International.

Far East Economic Review, 1994: *Asia 1994 Yearbook*. Hong Kong: Far East Economic Review Publishing Ltd.

Findlay, A. and Findlay, A. 1991: *Population and Development in the Third World*. London: Routledge.

Finkle, J. L. and McIntosh, C. A. (eds) 1994: *The New Politics of Population*. New York: The Population Council.

Flugel, J. C. 1947: *Population, Psychology and Peace*. London: Watts & Co.

Foote, K. A., Hill, K. H. and Martin, K. (eds) 1995: *Demographic Change in Sub-Saharan Africa*. Washington DC: National Academy Press.

Frankel, S. H. 1955: *Economic Impact on Underdeveloped Societies*. Oxford: Basil Blackwell.

Freedman, L. and Saunders, J. (eds) 1991: *Population Change and European Security*. London: Brassey's.

Grubb, M., Koch, M., Munson, A., Sullivan, F., and Thomson, K. 1993: *The Earth Summit Agreements: A Guide and Assessment*. London: Earthscan.

Hardin, G. 1993: *Living Within Limits: Ecology, Economics and Population Taboos*. New York: Oxford University Press.

Harrison, P. 1993: *The Third Revolution: Population, Environment and a Sustainable World*. London: Penguin.

Hartmann, B. 1987: *Reproductive Rights and Wrongs: The Global Politics of Population Control and Contraceptive Choice*. New York: Harper & Row.

Hauser, P. M. (ed.) 1969: *The Population Dilemma*. Englewood Cliffs, NJ: Prentice Hall.

Hawthorn, G. (ed.) 1978: *Population and Development*. London: Frank Cass.

Hertzler, J. O. 1956: *The Crisis in World Population: A Sociological Examination with Special Reference to the Undervdeveloped Areas*. Lincoln Nebraska: University of Nebraska Press.

Himmelfarb, M. and Baras, V. (eds) 1978: *Zero Population Growth. For Whom? Differential Fertility and Minority Group Survival*. Westport, Conn.: Greenwood Press.

Hjortafornas, A. and Salih, M. A. M. 1992: *Ecology and Politics: Environmental Stress and Security in Africa*. Motala, Sweden: Scandinavian Institute of African Studies.

HMSO, 1995: *Technology Foresight 4: Health and Life Sciences*. London: HMSO.

Hobsbawn, E. J. 1994: *Age of Extremes: The Short Twentieth Century 1914–1991*. London: Michael Joseph.

Hogben, L. (ed.) 1938: *Political Arithmetic: A Symposium of Population Studies*. London: George Allen & Unwin.

Hoselitz, B. F. (ed.) 1960: *Theories of Economic Growth*. Chicago: The Free Press of Glencoe.

Hunt, M. H. 1987: *Ideology and US Foreign Policy*. New Haven: Yale University Press.

Information Project for Africa (IPFA), 1991: *Population Control and National Security*. Washington DC: IPFA.

—— 1993a: *Propaganda, Cultural Imperialism and Population Control*. Washington DC: IPFA.

—— 1993b: *Ambassadors of Colonialism: the International Development Trap*. Washington DC: IPFA.

—— 1995: *Excessive Force: Power, Politics and Population Control*. Washington DC: IPFA.

Ingham, B. and Simmons, C. (eds) 1987: *Development Studies and Colonial Policy*. London: Frank Cass.

International Commission on Peace and Food. 1994: *Uncommon Opportunities: An Agenda for Peace and Equitable Development*. London: Zed Books.

Johnson, P. (ed.) 1994: *Twentieth Century Britain: Economic, Social, and Cultural Change*. London: Longman.

Johnson, S. P. 1987: *World Population and the United Nations: Challenge and

Response. Cambridge: Cambridge University Press.

Johnson, T. 1995: *A Vanishing People? Population, Fertility and Venereal Disease among the Ila of Northern Rhodesia, 1900–1960*. Lusaka: Unpublished paper, Institute for African Studies, University of Zambia.

Jones, G. 1980: *Social Darwinism and English Thought: The Interaction between Biological and Social Theory*. Brighton: Harvester Press.

—— 1996: *Social Hygiene in Twentieth Century Britain*. London: Croom Helm.

Kasun, J. 1988: *The War Against Population: The Economics and Ideology of Population Control*. San Francisco: Ignatius Press.

Kennedy, P. 1993: *Preparing for the Twenty-First Century*. London: Harper Collins.

Kirk, D. 1942: *The Fertility of the Negro*. Princeton: Office of Population Research.

—— 1946: *Europe's Population in the Interwar Years*. Princeton: Princeton University Press.

Kuczynski, R. R. 1948: *A Demographic Survey of the British Colonial Empire: Volume 1*. London: Oxford University Press.

Kuznets, S. 1966: *Economic Growth and Structure*: Selected Essays. London: Heinemann.

—— 1973: *Population, Capital and Growth: Selected Essays*. New York: W. W. Norton.

Lagemann, E. C. 1992: *The Politics of Knowledge: The Carnegie Corporation, Philanthrophy and Public Policy*. Chicago: University of Chicago Press.

Lee, R. D., Arthur, B., Kelley, A. C. and Srinivasan, T. N. (eds) 1988: *Population, Food and Rural Development*. Oxford: Clarendon Press.

Lewis, W. A. 1965: *The Theory of Economic Growth*. London: George Allen & Unwin. Originally published in 1955.

Lindahl-Kiessling, K. and Landberg, H. (eds) 1994: *Population, Economic Development and the Environment*. Oxford: Oxford University Press.

Linton, R. (ed.) 1945: *The Science of Man in the World Crisis*. New York: Columbia University.

Lorimer, F. and Osborn, F. 1934: *Dynamics of Population*. New York: Macmillan.

Love, G. A. and Love, R. M. (eds) 1970: *Ecological Crisis: Readings for Survival*. New York: Harcourt Brace Jovanovich.

Lutz, W. (ed.) 1994: *The Future Population of the World*. London: Earthscan.

Mahedevan, K. (ed.) 1989: *Women and Population Dynamics: Perspectives from Asian Countries*. New Delhi: Sage Publications.

Malthus, T. R. 1970: *An Essay on the Principle of Population*. Harmondsworth: Penguin Books.

Mass, B. 1976: *Population Target: The Political Economy of Population Control in Latin America*. Brampton, Ontario: Charters Publishing Co.

Meadows, D. H., Meadows, D. L. and Randers, J. 1992: *Beyond the Limits*. London: Earthscan.

Michaelson, K. L. (ed.) 1981: *And the Poor Get Children: Radical Perspectives on Population Dynamics*. New York: Monthly Review Press.

Milbank Memorial Fund (ed.) 1954: *The Interrelations of Demographic, Economic, and Social Problems in Selected Underdeveloped Areas*. New York: Milbank Memorial Fund.

Moore Lappé, F. and Schurman, R. 1989: *Taking population Seriously*. London: Earthscan.

Murray, C. 1990: *The Emerging British Underclass*. London: IEA.

Myrdal, G. 1962: *Population. A Problem for Democracy*. Gloucester, Mass.: Peter Smith.

Nair, S. 1989: *Imperialism and the Control of Women's Fertility*. London: Campaign Against Long-acting Hormonal Contraceptives.

National Research Council 1986: *Population Growth and Economic Development*. Washington DC: National Academy Press.

North, R. D. 1995: *Life on a Modern Planet: A Manifesto for Progress*. Manchester: Manchester University Press.

OECD, 1988: *Voluntary Aid for Development: The Role of NGOs*. Paris: OECD.

Overbeek, J. 1974: *History of Population Theories*. Rotterdam: Rotterdam University Press.

Pearson, L. B. 1969: *Report of the Commission on International Development*, London: Pall Mall Press.

Piotrow, P. T. 1973: *World Population Crisis: The United States Response*. New York: Praeger.

Rashid, A. 1994: *The Resurgence of Central Asia: Islam or Nationalism*. London: Zed Press.

Repetto, R. 1979: *Economic Equality and Fertility in Developing Countries*. Baltimore: Johns Hopkins University Press.

Riedmann, A. 1993: *Science that Colonizes: A Critique of Fertility Studies in Africa*. Philadelphia: Temple University Press.

Robbins, J. 1959: *Too Many Asians*. Garden City NY: Doubleday and Company.

Sachs, W. (ed.) 1992: *The Development Dictionary*. London: Zed Books.

Sauvy, A. 1969: *General Theory of Population*. London: Weidenfeld & Nicholson.

Sen, G., Germain, A., and Chen, L. C. (eds) 1994: *Population Policies Reconsidered: Health, Empowerment and Rights*. Boston: Harvard University Press.

Sen, G. and Grown, C. 1988: *Development, Crises and Alternative Visions: Third World Women's Perspectives*. London: Earthscan.

Simon, J. L. 1977: *The Economics of Population Growth*. Princeton: Princeton University Press.

—— 1981: *The Ultimate Resource*. Oxford: Martin Robertson.

—— 1986: *Theory of Population and Economic Growth*. Oxford: Basil Blackwell.

Spengler, J. J. and Duncan, O. D. (eds) 1956: *Population Theory and Policy: Selected Readings*. Glencoe, Illinois: The Free Press.

Sutherland, H. 1994: *Control of Life*. London: Burn, Oates & Washbourne Ltd.

Sweetman, C. (ed.) 1994: *Population and Reproductive Rights*. Oxford: Oxfam.

Symonds, R. and Carder, M. 1973: *The United Nations and the Population Question 1945–1960*. London: Sussex University Press.

Teitelbaum, M. S. and Winter, J. M. 1985: *The Fear of Population Decline*. Orlando, Florida: Academic Press.

—— (eds) 1989: *Population and Resources in Western Intellectual Traditions*. Cambridge: Cambridge University Press.

Thompson, E. T. (ed.) 1939: *Race Relations and the Race Problem*. Durham, North Carolina: Duke University Press.

Thompson, W. S. 1929: *Danger Spots in World Population*. New York: Alfred A. Knopf.

—— 1946: *Population and Peace in the Pacific*. Chicago: University of Chicago Press.

Tiffen, M., Mortimore, M. and Gichuki, F. 1994: *More People, Less Erosion:*

Environmental Recovery in Kenya. Chichester: John Wiley & Sons.

Todaro, M. P. 1989: *Economic Development in the Third World*. New York: Longman.

Turner, B. L., Hyden, G., and Kates, R. W. (eds) 1993: *Population Growth and Agricultural Change in Africa*. Gainesville, Florida: University Press of Florida.

Turner, C. H. 1923: *Public Opinion and World Peace*. Washington DC: ILCA.

United Nations. 1953: *The Determinants and Consequences of Population Growth: A Summary of the Findings of Studies on the Relationship between Population Changes and Economic and Social Conditions*. New York: UN.

—— 1988: *World Population: Trends and Policies. 1987 Monitoring Report*. New York: UN.

—— 1994: *World Economic and Social Survey 1994*. New York: UN.

United Nations Population Fund, 1995: *The State of World Population 1995*. New York: UNFPA.

Vogt, W. 1949: *Road to Survival*. London: Victor Gollanz.

Warwick, D. P. 1987: *Bitter Pills: Population Policies and their Implementation in Eight Developing Countries*. Cambridge: Cambridge University Press.

Wattenberg, B. 1987: *The Birth Dearth*. New York: Pharos Book.

Webb, S. 1907: *The Decline in the Birth Rate*. London: Fabian Society.

Weigert, H. 1947: *Generals and Geographers: The Twilight of Geopolitics*. London: Oxford University Press.

Wilson, C. (ed.) 1985: *The Dictionary of Demography*. Oxford: Basil Blackwell.

World Bank, 1974: *Population Policies and Economic Development*. Baltimore: Johns Hopkins University Press.

—— 1984: *World Development Report*. Washington DC: Oxford University Press.

—— 1995: *Global Economic Prospects and the Developing Countries*. Washington DC: The World Bank.

World Commission on Environment and Development, 1987: *Our Common Future*. Oxford: Oxford University Press.

Worsley, P. (ed.) 1987: *Introducing the New Sociology*. Harmondsworth: Penguin.

Wright, F. C. (ed.) 1939: *Population and Peace: A Survey of International Opinion on Claims for Relief from Population Pressure*. Paris: League of Nations.

Index